Two week loan

Please return on or before the last date stamped below.
Charges are made for late return.

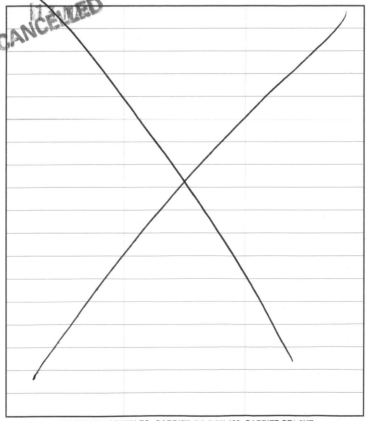

Buying and Clearing Rights

Buying and Clearing Rights

Print, broadcast and multimedia

Richard McCracken and
Madeleine Gilbart

BLUEPRINT
An Imprint of Chapman & Hall

London · Glasgow · Weinheim · New York · Tokyo · Melbourne · Madras

Published by Blueprint, an imprint of Chapman & Hall, 2–6 Boundary Row, London SE1 8HN, UK

Chapman & Hall, 2–6 Boundary Row, London SE1 8HN, UK

Blackie Academic & Professional, Wester Cleddens Road, Bishopbriggs, Glasgow G64 2NZ, UK

Chapman & Hall GmbH, Pappelallee 3, 69469 Weinheim, Germany

Chapman & Hall USA, 115 Fifth Avenue, New York, NY 10003, USA

Chapman & Hall Japan, ITP-Japan, Kyowa Building, 3F, 2-2-1 Hirakawacho, Chiyoda-ku, Tokyo 102, Japan

Chapman & Hall Australia, 102 Dodds Street, South Melbourne, Victoria 3205, Australia

Chapman & Hall India, R. Seshadri, 32 Second Main Road, CIT East, Madras 600 035, India

First edition 1995

© 1995 Richard McCracken and Madeleine Gilbart

Typeset in Times 10/12pt by Saxon Graphics Ltd, Derby

Printed in Great Britain by T.J. Press (Padstow) Ltd., Padstow, Cornwall

ISBN 1 85713 025 1

∞ Printed on acid-free text paper, manufactured in accordance with ANSI/NISO Z39.48-1992 (Permanence of Paper).

Contents

Foreword

Twenty years ago the only people who really took an interest in copyright law and the clearing of intellectual property rights were publishers, record companies, broadcasters and their lawyers. It was, and still is, part of the territory of their business and professional training.

Things have now changed radically and irreversibly. The technological means to create works for publication in print, broadcast and multimedia have moved from the industrial estate to the desktop. Almost anyone can now become a publisher – and why not? But open a box containing the latest desktop publishing technology and there will be precious few instructions included to inform the owner about clearing the rights to make use of works created or owned by other people.

This book has been written to fill that gap. It has been encouraged into print by the British Universities Film & Video Council and Heather Rosenblatt of the Composers' Guild of Great Britain, following a series of conferences and one-day courses on copyright which have demonstrated a real demand for information in this field.

Copyright law is one thing, but the day-to-day business arrangements which operate within the legislation are quite another. The authors of *Buying and Clearing Rights,* Richard McCracken and Madeleine Gilbart, have gained their experience through work for specialist rights clearance departments in the Open University and the BBC. The Open University in the UK, which now has a track-record extending over 25 years, has experience which is second to none in publishing across a wide range of media.

Recent announcements of the death of copyright, by certain parties with an interest in the wider use of information technology, are surely premature if not totally naive. This book goes some way to ensuring that its readers will have an opportunity to operate within the established conventions of the publishing business and not risk sleepless nights, if not their personal fortunes, through ignorance.

Murray Weston
Director
British Universities Film & Video Council

Acknowledgements

We would like to acknowledge and thank Bernadette Attwell, Rights Assistant at the Open University; David Harding, Senior Contracts Executive at the BBC; Heather Rosenblatt, General Secretary of the Composers' Guild of Great Britain and lecturer in IP law; Hugo Sakkers, Legal Adviser, Philips Europe; Murray Weston, Director of the British Universities Film and Video Council; and colleagues in the Rights department of the Open University for all their advice, patience and help in writing this book.

Figures 1.1, 1.2 and 1.3 are reproduced courtesy of the Open University.

Introduction

This book has been written as a practical guide for anyone concerned with the acquisition and clearance of intellectual property rights in the course of producing or compiling their own material. It is aimed at broadcast and multimedia producers, software developers, educational developers and providers, and publishers – anyone who encounters the difficulties of clearing rights against the constraints of tight budgets and looming deadlines. It is not intended to be an academic study or a legal textbook and should not be taken to be an authoritative legal analysis of copyright law. Its concerns lie with the practical application of copyright law as applied to the practical concerns faced every day by those seeking to clear third party material for inclusion in the course of production, particularly multimedia production. It is written from the producer's or user's point of view, taking account of the sometimes isolated business of dealing with rights clearance, and seeks to provide the sort of practical advice, born of experience, that everyone working in an often unfamiliar field would choose to have at their side. This is not to say that the real and legitimate concerns of rights holders are not considered, for at the heart of the book's approach to rights clearance there is a sense of fairness and of agreement being arrived at through open negotiation. It does, however, mean that some of the opinions expressed would not necessarily be shared by all whose rights the producer will seek to acquire or license. Inexperienced producers or those entering into production for the first time should not be tempted to think that underlying rights holders have little say in negotiations with producers.

The book has been structured so that it can be read both as an accumulated overview of copyright and rights clearance and as a series of integrated chapters dealing with the complexities of clearing specific media in detail. It builds from setting copyright in context to guidance on developing rights clearance strategies for multimedia production, yet will allow easy access to advice on specific areas as they arise in the course of production.

It is important to be able to develop an overview of copyright and rights in context because rights clearance in new media can sometimes be complicated by our sense of excitement at the opportunities offered by the technology itself. The ability to break down and analyse the rights position as a series of basic building blocks is an important transferrable skill that will apply equally to new technologies as they come on line. The book's approach throughout is that the effective clearance of rights is a function of proper production planning. The more that rights clearance can be incorporated as an essential and early function of the production process, the more widely the 'product' can, in the end, be distributed and exploited.

Copyright in context 1

This chapter is not a detailed examination of copyright law. Just the same, the buying and selling of rights does not exist exclusively in a purely practical world of production scheduling and rights negotiation. It demands to be set in an appropriate legal context, namely the origins of copyright and what it is that copyright and related rights protect.

On one level, of course, the situation is self-evident. Copyright is a right that allows its owner to grant or withhold the right to make copies. But who controls the right and which works are protected? Here we come to the split in attitude between those who view copyright as a means of protecting and encouraging creativity and those who see it as a property right to be developed and exploited within a commercial environment. The two views are not, of course, mutually exclusive. Most artists would be only too happy to receive proper commercial returns from their creative work and would be capable of even greater creativity if only they were able to live more comfortably; equally, most publishers share a deep interest in succouring and promoting the creativity of their writers. In the UK and other common law countries, such as the US, copyright is viewed as a property right and like all forms of property in a commercial environment it exists to be bought and sold.

What copyright protects, therefore, is the ability of its owner to control its exploitation. This means, in turn, that if a production is going to include material taken from other sources (third party copyright material) then the producer is faced with the following decisions:

- Is the material protected by copyright?
- Is there a defence against infringement which allows for use without clearing?
- How best to clear it?
- Who controls it?

1.1 PROTECTED MATERIAL

Copyright protects the physical expression of an idea, not the idea itself, and is achieved at the point of expression, without registration. While a copyright work is being created as this chapter is written, someone speaking at a presentation may have no copyright in their ad lib remarks simply because they have no fixation, no physical record of those remarks. On the other hand, speaking from brief notes would be sufficient for a speaker to acquire copyright. In that case subsequent copying would be in breach of copyright unless permission had been granted.

What categories of work may be protected by copyright? As we have seen, no registration is necessary and neither need the work be original, in the sense of being able to pass any threshold of creativity or inventiveness. That is the European notion. In the UK, originality as applied to a copyright work simply refers to there being an identifiable author with whom the work originated. The work itself may be of the most mundane nature and still be protected, for example a railway timetable.

The author, as the originator of the work, becomes the original owner of the copyright in the work and has the right to sell or license the right to control the acts restricted by copyright. The restricted acts, which infringe the copyright of the copyright owner unless undertaken by permission, include:

- copying the work;
- issuing copies to the public;
- performing, showing or playing the work in public;
- broadcasting or distributing the work via cable;
- making an adaptation of the work (and also doing any of the restricted acts with the adaptation itself).

While in most cases the author of the work and owner of copyright is taken to be the person first creating the work, certain exceptions apply, principally in the case of works created by employees in the course of their employment. Copyright in that case is vested in the employer.

In works of joint authorship, copyright is shared in cases where the contributions of the authors cannot be distinguished one from the other. Separate copyright may be agreed where each author makes a discrete contribution that can be clearly identified. Other collaborative works are treated differently, though, and the most important of these for consideration here are films and television programmes, for which the producer is held to be the author.

Works protected by copyright fall into the following main categories: literary, dramatic, musical and artistic works; sound recordings; films; broadcasts and cable programmes and typographical arrangements. It is possible for multimedia productions to strain some of these definitions and there is a continuing dialogue at both national and international level about the extent to which copyright legislation may require amendment. The introduction of new rights, most notably a digital diffusion right, is under consideration but the extent to which copyright law may yet be amended is unclear.

Before going on to look at each briefly in turn, it is important to understand that some of these terms carry an artistic cachet in everyday usage that does not apply to copyright. Literary works need have no literary merit and neither need dramatic works be acclaimed, nor musical works be hummable nor artistic works the products of tortured genius.

1.1.1 LITERARY WORKS

Literary works are defined negatively. They are works which are neither musical nor dramatic works (although they may be written, spoken or sung). The category includes tables, compilations and, significantly, computer programmes, though computer software does have some particular provisions which do not apply to other forms of literary work. As a result, charts and compilations may be copyright as literary works in their own right. In practice, this means that quoting a single chart or table from a book requires clearance because they are assessed as complete and separate works in their own right, not as minor or insubstantial parts of the whole book. It also means that the compilation or selection of a set of tables, or an anthology of poetry, for example, may be protected by copyright, even though the facts may be in the public domain or the poems out of copyright, so that reproduction of a substantial part of the compiled work would be an infringement of the author's right in the compilation.

1.1.2 DRAMATIC WORKS

This category includes plays, obviously, but it also covers other physical activities which may be fixed or recorded, including works of dance or mime. The act of recording or fixing includes recording in writing (such as choreographic notation) or on film or tape or by any other technological means. Choreographic notes are themselves classified as literary works. It is the work produced as a result of following the notes' directions that is protected as a dramatic work.

1.1.3 MUSICAL WORKS

The musical work is, as you might guess, 'a work consisting of music' and is treated separately from any accompanying lyrics or dance movement. It is protected as soon as it is fixed, whether by writing, musical notation or other means. It includes musical directions, which are taken to form part of the score.

1.1.4 ARTISTIC WORKS

Artistic works fall into three categories:

1. That which most closely corresponds to what we generally think of as 'artistic', covering graphic works, photographs, sculptures and collages.
2. Works of architecture and architectural models.
3. Works of artistic craftsmanship.

This third category is a rather confused one which, unusually in UK legislation, does take some account of an imagined quality threshold as a requirement for protection. A roughly constructed prototype frame for a piece of furniture, for example, has been held not to have been of sufficient craftsmanship to acquire protection. A crafted designer chair, on the other hand, would.

1.1.5 SOUND RECORDINGS

A sound recording is a recording on any medium or the method by which sounds may be reproduced or produced. The recording may be of a musical, literary or dramatic work or simply be of other recognizable sounds, such as street noises, sound effects, or whatever. It is separate from any copyright existing in the work being recorded, so that a recording of music will be entitled to copyright as a recording in its own right but may also contain further rights held in the music, lyrics, arrangement and performance.

1.1.6 FILMS

Films are defined as a recording on any medium from which a moving image may be reproduced by any means. They do not, as a category, include the film soundtrack (a sound recording) or any other component which goes to make up the complete film as a body of work. As a result, if you wish to incorporate into your production an extract from a film or television programme or corporate video, you will have to take account of any other copyright elements contained in the original: soundtrack, script, performances and lyrics.

1.1.7 BROADCASTS AND CABLE TRANSMISSIONS

These two are categorized separately, which means that broadcast rights in a programme intended for transmission do not cover subsequent cable distribution. Those rights are held to be separate. However, broadcast and cable rights might usefully be discussed together when considering broadcast production.

Broadcasts are transmissions by means of wireless telegraphy of programmes which are freely available for reception by members of the public. In the same way that sound recordings are protected separately from the information they record, so broadcasts are protected separately from the programmes they carry. Except for the purposes of time-shifting by making ephemeral recordings for home use, recording a broadcast off-air infringes the rights of both broadcaster and programme maker, as well as rights held by other contributors to the programme. The Copyright, Designs and Patents Act 1988 also makes provision for the free recording of broadcast programmes by educational establishments subject to two conditions: the recordings must be for the educational purposes of the institution and they may be made without payment only to the extent that no registered licensing scheme exists to license the recordings. In practice, the majority of recordings are covered by two licensing schemes representing the major broadcasters, the unions and the Open University but not all broadcast material is covered by the schemes and so may be recorded by educational establishments without licence.

Encrypted programming is still held to be a broadcast if the means of decoding the transmission is made freely available to the public. A totally encoded transmission not meant for reception by the public is not a broadcast, for example private communication lines between the sites of a multinational company.

Cable transmission is not made by means of wireless telegraphy, depending as it does upon there being a cable (a wire) in place. Like a broadcast, though, it is capable of protection separately from the programming it carries.

1.1.8 PUBLISHED EDITIONS

In effect, copyright protection of published editions gives publishers the copyright in the typeface and layout of their works.

It is common for quotes from out-of-copyright works to be used as camera ready copy or to be scanned in as part of the production process. In either case, the effect is the absolute reproduction of the original typeface and layout of the book from which the quote is taken. It is easy to assume that, because the work itself is out of copyright, no infringement can take place – forgetting that the publisher's rights in the published edition lasts for 25 years from the year of publication. If you are using a published edition as camera ready copy or scanning it in within 25 years of its publication, clearance will be needed.

Published editions of out-of-copyright works are often 'wrapped around' with modern introductions, glossaries of terms, etc. and these will be subject to copyright in their own right.

1.2 THE EUROPEAN PERSPECTIVE

European Union directives on harmonizing copyright and associated legislation across all member states have implications for producers and publishers alike.

For many member states, the chief change to existing copyright legislation came in July 1995 when the term of copyright increased from 50 years after the death of the author to 70 years after the death of the author or, in the case of works of joint authorship, 70 years after the death of the last surviving author.

This seems likely to cause particular problems in the case of film and television, where the term of copyright will expire 70 years after the death of any one of a number of possible collaborating authors. Keeping track of the director, producer, scriptwriter, composer and lyricist, 70 or more years after the film was produced, will take some doing.

Publishers and broadcasters in the UK, for instance, also face having to deal with the re-qualification of out-of-copyright works as they come back into protection. Harmonization will be to the greatest level of protection applied in any one of the member states. Copyright protection will be granted to a work in all member states if it is capable of protection in any one.

Another important change comes as a result of the EU Draft Directive on Databases. This proposes a new European right protecting all databases from unauthorized or unfair extraction for a period of 15 years after construction. This applies to databases regardless of whether their individual entries are copyright or not. The Directive will also impose a new threshold of originality in the selection or arrangement if a database is to receive protection.

1.3 COPYRIGHT AND RIGHTS

This chapter attempts to look at legislation along practical lines and we have spent some time looking at the legal position of each category of protected work in turn. In doing so, it should have become clear that because works are protected according to category there exists the possibility of several different categories of work being contained in a single production. A recording of a popular song will contain a musical work (the score), a literary work (the lyrics) and a sound recording (the recording company's copyright in the recording). A television production of a theatrical play will contain a musical work (the score of the theme tune), a literary work (the theme lyrics), one or possibly two dramatic works (the television script and the original theatrical script from which it is adapted), a sound recording (the recording of the speech and, possibly, theme music available as a commercial recording), a film (the recorded visual performance) and a broadcast (the transmission of the programme).

The subdivision of works into protected categories reflects a similar division among various industries. This division becomes more muddled with the introduction of a multimedia environment in which the difference between the categories of the computing, book publishing, broadcasting and film-making industries is increasingly blurred. These technological fractures between industries still exist and may do so for some time yet. It brings about an important psychological effect upon the business of clearing and acquiring rights because each industry has its own rights culture, which may not sit easily with the needs or requirements of another medium. Each has its own way of dividing the world into territorial and marketing opportunities, each licenses on terms according to its own conventions and each has its own attitudes towards preserving (or not) the integrity of the work. All of this results in confusion when third party copyright material is licensed for use in a multimedia production.

While copyright can be bought or sold in its entirety, it rarely is. Most commonly the original author will either license the various rights in the work separately (rather as a cake may be sold as a series of slices) or authorize a publisher or broadcaster to license the rights on the author's behalf.

Using the 'cake' analogy, the rights 'slices' are defined by three-dimensional cuts. The slices are cut by negotiation between the rights holder and the licensee, using as a knife the interaction of copyright law with the laws of contract and licensing.

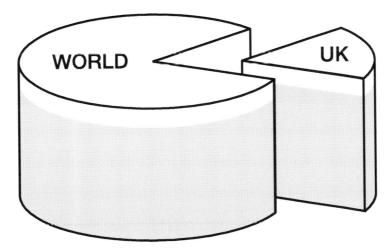

Figure 1.1 The rights slice

1.3.1 TERRITORIES

The simplest way of making the initial slice of the cake is territorial (Figure 1.1). It is common for the world to be split territorially with non-exclusive or exclusive licensing agreements granting rights for a particular territory (or group of territories). Common territorial divisions or groupings are: World; the UK; the European Union or, simply, Europe (giving a wider territorial spread); Middle East; Far East or Asia; North and/or South America; and, for UK publishers especially, the British Commonwealth. Digital technology means that territorial divisions are less useful than they were for analogue media. It is difficult to license by territory when a satellite footprint spills across several territories and has fringe reception in several more, or when material is made available on the Internet or World Wide Web. Another common definition of rights is 'World (excluding North America)' because for many products the North American market represents more than half of the world market. A publisher who does not intend dealing in North America could make a saving of more than 50% of rights clearance costs by not buying North American rights.

The list is clearly not exhaustive and the countries of eastern Europe and Africa are obvious omissions. It is possible to cater for particular projects by putting together other groupings. In doing so rights departments may take into account the economic similarities between countries and not rely solely upon geographical convenience. Most economically powerful countries existing in a close geographical proximity to other less powerful nations are singled out as territories in their own right. South Africa is a case in point, as are others among the countries of the former Soviet Union and eastern Europe.

1.3.2 RIGHTS WITHIN TERRITORIES

Exclusive agreements grant the licensee the exclusive right to a particular form of exploitation within the specified territory and prevent even the licensor from exploiting those same rights in competition. A non-exclusive licence, often used in licensing extracts of a work, allows the licensor the option of granting similar rights to others operating within the same territorial slice.

Remove the UK as a territorial slice of the cake and look more closely at the rights that might be cut from the copyright in that territory. The process could be repeated for other territories.

A book is a copyright work in which the publisher has been granted certain rights in consideration of payments made under contract. Look at the territorial slice from Figure 1.2. The medium in which the book exists is print but it might equally have been created as a television programme, film,

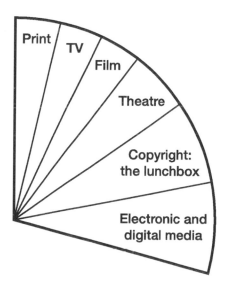

Figure 1.2   The territory/media slice, viewed from above

theatrical play or in electronic or digital formats, such as a networked system. The copyright owner might also be interested in creating and marketing products based upon or drawn from the characters in the book.

1.3.3 MEDIA OPTIONS

Whichever of these media options is chosen, a work is created capable of exploitation in a variety of ways, each representing an opportunity to license a fresh exploitation. In fact, the publisher may exercise rights on behalf of the author, including the presentation of the work via electronic means, but equally the author may have negotiated a contract that excludes the publisher from selling television or film rights in the work, retaining those under direct authorial control. Lunch-boxes and pencil-cases based on this book, soft toys and the associated paraphernalia of modern tie-in marketing will, of course, be in a shop near you soon.

Figure 1.3 examines this third dimension of the territorial slice. The knife shown in the figure represents the terms of the licence. This vertical slicing of the territorial division runs across all media and shows that, in licensing, how the work reaches its audience can count for as much as the medium itself. At a comparatively simple level, even though the end result is still a reader opening a book, the right to deliver the book to the reader may be subdivided into the various rights of paperback or hardback and book club or

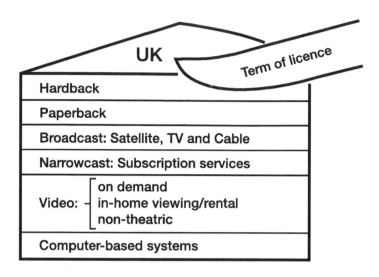

Figure 1.3   Territorial layers of exploitation

cheap editions. Delivery via electronic or networked systems, photocopying rights and translation rights are also licensed separately, though in some cases the publisher may handle these rights on behalf of the author.

For works that are produced in a more sophisticated technical environment (television productions, films, computer-based works, etc.), the rights available to licensing options become equally sophisticated. While, again, the end result may appear to be the same for all delivery systems – with a viewer watching a picture on screen – how the picture comes to reach the screen offers licensors every opportunity to slice their copyright ever more thinly and lucratively. A television programme, to take a common example, may be licensed for terrestrial broadcast. Should the producer or broadcaster wish to licence for distribution on cable, cable rights will have to be acquired too. Satellite transmission, again, will require a new level of clearance.

A market may also exist for sales of the programme on video – the rights for which may be licensed separately from the right to sell via CD – and the licensor may wish to take into account the point of sale. Retail sale for home use will be licensed separately from sale to educational institutions and neither will cover the rights necessary to screen the programme to a paying audience (the theatrical rights). The principle to understand clearly here is that copyright is often talked about in rather loose terms, particularly by those coming to it in the course of production. The empty and confusing phrase 'world rights' is often used rather carelessly to mean that the producer has acquired the right to use all contributions in all markets for all purposes, without hindrance. In fact, while the term may define the territory it says nothing about which rights are to be cleared within that world territory. Copyright is not an indivisible entity which needs clearing once and once only; it may be subdivided into an almost infinite number of rights, each of which is cleared or licensed through a process of negotiation between licensors and licensees.

This imposes a requirement upon every producer who chooses to use third party material in a production. Rights clearance must be an integral part of the production process if it is not to restrict the end exploitation of the programme. The rights in any production may only be exploited to the extent of its most restricted element. Leaving rights clearance to the last, frantic days of a production is asking for trouble. Leaving it until the product is released is asking for even more. By far the best and most constructive way of handling rights clearance is to make it an essential part of the forward production process. Use it to help focus upon the objective of making the programme or writing the book. Begin by asking the questions: 'Just why is this work being made? What do we hope to get out of it? Who or what is the intended audience? How are we going to reach them? Where?'

In asking such questions you will be doing more than focusing the production more tightly upon its intended audience and marketing targets. You will be saving time and money (and in production the two are often synonymous) by acquiring the rights you require, tailored exactly to the needs of the production, and you will be doing so at a time that leaves you in a more effective negotiating position. Leave rights clearance too late and you will be in a weak position to negotiate. Then losing a particular piece of third party material will leave you facing expensive re-editing or, worse still, having to reconstruct the entire project against impossible deadlines. This is particularly so with educational or other self-referencing works in which a small piece of third party material may be the meeting point of many cross-references from a great deal of supporting material.

1.4 THE IMPACT OF TECHNOLOGY

We are concerned with the clearing of rights in a fast-changing technological environment. It helps to anticipate a production's future rights requirements and so develop a rights clearance strategy that will extend the useful working life of a production into other markets and through other technologies. To understand that, we need to recognize that the interaction of copyright and rights has always been driven by technological developments. From the advent of cheap mass-market printing in the nineteenth century to present developments in computer-based and electronic media, copyright legislation has had to evolve to survive. Industry practices have kept pace, sometimes surviving long after the technological imperatives which created them. For example, it is common practice for actors to be paid repeat fees for subsequent transmission of productions in which they perform. This practice first arose at a time when television recording was in its infancy and the repeat of Sunday evening's episode of a popular drama meant that the cast gathered again on the evening of the repeat and went through the whole performance again. In this case, industrial practice was led by technological restrictions. By the time technology improved and filmed or videotaped repeats were possible, the practice had become established and remains so. Whether it will remain in the face of newer financial and technological pressures remains to be seen.

There is no benefit in examining the new technologies in so much detail at this point that it detracts from later chapters where the particular rights characteristics of each medium, particularly multimedia, will be examined in a proper context. However, the ways in which new and emerging technologies drive together the media of broadcasting, publishing and software has an enormous impact on our thinking in clearing rights for productions.

The question facing rights acquisitions at a time of change is, therefore, how to cut clearance costs in production and still keep open options for future exploitation. The ideal is to clear as widely as possible while incurring minimum cost and there are three main ways of achieving this: buy-outs (below), residuals (p.13) and royalties (p.13).

In practice you should expect to use a mix of all three methods. Rights holders in different media calculate their income according to the practice of their industry. Actors, musicians and other professional broadcasters expect royalty payments and there is a definite move towards royalty-based payments and away from residuals in productions which use a lot of union contributors. Film libraries, on the other hand, generally calculate payment as a percentage of the original fee; often they refuse options entirely and insist upon renegotiation for each exploitation. Music (both commercial and library) tends to operate on a once-only payment, though the sales may be restricted to a particular licensing limit.

1.4.1 BUY-OUTS

For some kinds of material and certain contributors it is possible to offer a one-off fee which acquires all rights in the material or contribution across all media in perpetuity. A buy-out like this is the most effective and, ultimately, most cost-effective way of ensuring that the material is cleared for use, whatever the future plans for the production. It can be used to acquire at low cost all rights in small contributions such as people interviewed in the street, owners of family photographs and other ephemera, some kinds of commissioned music and short written contributions.

It is difficult to apply, though, to union contributors and others who rely on the exercise of intellectual property rights for their livelihood, or to commercial photo or footage libraries, museums, galleries and the like. If a rights holder in one of these professional categories does consent to a buy-out, it is likely to be at a higher than usual fee or a percentage supplement paid in addition to the standard rate, and then generally for certain rights, not all. At that point you must decide if the higher fee is cost efficient; that is, are you going to make full use of the range of rights you have acquired or is the additional cost of the buy-out wasted on rights that will be underexploited?

Where the buy-out scores is in its cutting away of administrative costs. Even though relatively small items of third party material are unlikely to cause delay and will not be expensive to re-clear, the administrative time and effort involved in keeping track of small contributions and writing to each rights holder for permission can become expensive.

For more substantial rights holders you are unlikely to achieve a buy-out. In that case you should take options on those rights you do not need for the primary exploitation of the work. Options are, in effect, a form of deferred payment. They guarantee that the rights are available when the opportunity for secondary exploitation arises but commit you to no further payment unless the option is exercised. There are two ways of guaranteeing options: residuals and royalties. Both have their advantages.

1.4.2 RESIDUALS

Residuals are payments to contributors calculated as a percentage of the rights holder's original fee. They can be a comparatively cheap way of paying for exploitation within a particular territory and carry a low administrative cost. They can, though, go badly wrong if sales are lower than expected. In that case residual payments could possibly be greater than net income.

1.4.3 ROYALTIES

Royalties are payments calculated as a percentage either of the sale price or, preferably, of net income arising from sales of the product. They carry a greater administrative cost and can result in larger payments being made to rights holders but do have the advantage of being directly related to income. Properly set up, you only pay out if you are making a profit.

1.5 DEFENCES AGAINST INFRINGEMENT

Having spent some time examining material to be cleared for use and the ways and means of clearing it, what about material that can be used without clearance? What defences are available which make it possible to quote copyright material without permission and without payment?

The two most commonly used defences against infringement, aside from the obvious defence that the material is either out of copyright or has been placed in the public domain, rely upon fair dealing for the purposes of criticism or review and the insubstantiality of the extract being quoted. Both carry a requirement to acknowledge fully and properly the source and copyright holder of the material.

1.5.1 FAIR DEALING

Although known almost unquestioningly as 'fair dealing', the complete wording of the defence must be broken down fully into its component parts if it is to be interpreted properly. It allows for the quoting of copyright material under the defence of "fair dealing for the purposes of criticism or review". The phrase is balanced and hinges upon two requirements. The first is that the use of the material must be fair. The second is that the defence is valid only if the use is for criticism or review. It is not enough, therefore, to publish an entire novel and claim fair dealing as a defence simply by saying, 'I enjoyed this book' at the foot of the last page. That would clearly be unfair to the copyright owner (and would hardly qualify either as criticism or review).

On the other hand, there is no restriction on the amount of a work that may be quoted, save that it must be the minimum possible for the purposes of making the criticism or review. One case, for example, centred on a book which promoted a scientific method of winning the football pools. A letter was published in a weekly pools forecasting journal in which a reader quoted an important section of the scientific method, showing how stakes might be placed for maximum benefit. The letter compared this original table with another of a different type, giving reasons for preferring one over the other. Though it was agreed that a substantial part of the original work had been quoted without permission, the court held that the letter writer and the publisher of the journal in which it appeared had not infringed copyright in comparing the two tables.

1.5.2 INSUBSTANTIAL PART

If it is an infringement of copyright to copy or adapt, etc. a substantial part of a copyright work, it must follow that copying cannot be an infringement if the quote is an insubstantial part. The question of substantiality is often confused with a factual measurement of length or duration. This is not so.

The substantiality of a quoted extract is measured by its value, significance or importance in relation to the work as a whole. This has some interesting results. Several pages or more taken from a book might well not be considered substantial, yet a few paragraphs disclosing the identity of the murderer in a whodunit might well be. Everything depends on the importance of the part to the whole.

It is almost impossible to quote more than a few lines of poetry or notes of music without infringing by quoting a substantial part. This is because it is held that the words in poetry, or the notes in music, have to 'fight to be included' (sections 4.1.6 and 4.1.7).

To assess quoted extracts from textual material a useful guide may be the Publishers Association guidelines for UK publishers. This suggests that around 400 words of continuous prose may be quoted without clearance. The figure rises to 800 if the quote is not continuous (providing that no single section is longer than 300 words) For quotes from newspaper and journal articles and other short prose works, the guidelines suggest that either 400 words or 10% of the complete article is reasonable, whichever is the shorter.

These figures are no more than guidelines generally accepted within the UK publishing industry. They are meant for ease of use and are not definitive rulings. Every case must be judged on its merit and the ability to do that comes with experience. The guidelines are offered only in the spirit of a brief shortcut towards experience.

This is particularly the case with information displayed in graphic formats, such as tables, charts, graphs and maps. As copyright protects the physical expression of the information, not the information itself, how much of the graphic can be used without infringing? Again, the defences of fair dealing and insubstantiality must be applied in ways similar to prose quotes. In addition, though, there remains the option of redrawing the figure so substantially that no infringement occurs. This is not an option to take without thought because the redrawn version will still be an infringing adaptation of the original if it incorporates a substantial part of the original. You have to examine your own motives in making the redrawn version. Are you doing the redrawing in order to express the information better or are you attempting to avoid copyright fees rightfully due? This sense of fairness is a constantly useful yardstick with which to measure any case in which you are uncertain. A sense of fairness is essential to the copyright system as it operates in practice. Without the sense of trust that is generated between rights holders and users the entire structure founders, particularly at a time when technology makes unrestricted, untraceable copying so much easier than ever before.

Co-productions and collaborative productions

2

The high administrative and clearance costs associated with using third party copyright in multimedia production and the wide-ranging skills required by the production team is increasingly driving producers towards collaborative production. For rights holders controlling archives of footage, programming, stills and text, collaborative production offers a means of releasing or enhancing the value of the assets held in the archive. For production companies, broadcasters, software houses and other multimedia developers, access to archive material offers an alternative to the painstaking and expensive business of clearing many hundreds of individual items of third-party copyright material. Collaborative ventures are an especially attractive option for many educational institutions who have a great deal of expertise to offer, particularly at the cutting edges of new technologies and in higher level educational development, but who have neither the production experience nor the financial backing to enter production alone. Collaboration for them may be in consortia made up of many other similar institutions, or a mixture of educational institutions and commercial developers, or with commercial interests alone.

For many, initial enthusiasm can turn quickly to confrontation as the collaborating partners argue about marketing and development rights. Almost invariably such arguments result from a failure to draw up proper collaborative contracts before work on the collaboration starts in earnest. By means of these formal preliminaries, the issues of rights ownership and the splitting of responsibilities for development and marketing and the returns on marketing may be decided in advance. This is important: firstly, because negotiation is often more productive and valuable at times of less pressure and secondly because, once work commences, copyright materials start to be created. In the absence of any umbrella agreement to the contrary, copyright in individual segments of work will rest with the initiating institution, not with the project. Even where one member of the consortium has collaborated closely with another in developing the concepts behind the development, it may be that a third member actually puts those ideas into physical shape – and copyright lies in the expression of an idea, not the idea itself.

The first step in any collaboration must be, therefore, the drafting of an agreement taking care of the intellectual property rights created in the venture. Apart from taking care of rights issues that will, without fail, arise later, this also carries the benefit of forcing the collaborators to firm up their ideas and look seriously at the questions of which partner does what, how the project is to be managed and how it is intended to be exploited. For many collaborators, the project is initiated between friends and momentum grows until there comes a time when work is started without formal agreement having been reached. With some consortia in education having memberships approaching 50 institutions, this is a recipe for chaos – if not disaster.

The development of a successful multimedia strategy depends upon the recognition that multimedia as we understand it represents a convergence of many industries, each with differing traditions of expertise and experience. The new multimedia industries are at such an early stage of development, and multimedia production itself requires such a spread of expertise, that it makes sense to hedge one's bets by collaborating across several projects with collaborators from a range of backgrounds in publishing, broadcasting, computing and telecommunications. Hardware and software standards are still in a state of flux. Will the industry that emerges most closely mirror the experiences of publishing or broadcasting, or software development or telecommunication? If the VHS/Betamax battle for the video market is a guide, the broad acceptance of one standard rather than another will depend on the hardware manufacturers' ability to keep costs down and the ability of multimedia producers and software developers to present a huge range of titles, rather than necessarily upon the better technical capabilities of the platform.

Issues of intellectual property and licensing are particularly important for collaborations in multimedia. These fall into three categories: licensing, ownership and control. They are often separate and are often confused.

2.1 RIGHTS IN THE COLLABORATIVE PRODUCT

2.1.1 LICENSING

Because of the nature of multimedia development, collaborative production is often driven by the need of the partners to have access to a body of source materials free from rights clearance costs, or at least easily available at low cost. The materials must be available for exploitation throughout the world and in all media, unless the project is very specifically aimed at a small target audience in one territory. This is increasingly unlikely. In order to achieve this, intellectual property rights in materials developed in production are vested in the project, whether they are developed in the course of production by one or other of the collaborators or by the project jointly. Provision should be made for the equitable splitting of rights upon expiry of the collaboration agreement or on termination. Existing materials brought to the project by the partners will be supplied to the project under licence, for the purpose of the project's core business. Determining exactly what that core business is can be difficult, particularly for multimedia projects where the market is in evolution. The current state of the market may be difficult to define and future trends difficult to forecast. However, the exercise itself is a useful way of working towards a focus for the project.

2.1.2 OWNERSHIP

Partners in collaborative projects often place great importance in negotiating ownership of copyright, confusing ownership with the ability to act. It is often more productive to avoid focusing on the question of ownership and instead to talk about the ability to exploit the rights arising out of copyright. The rights to use and exploit the material commercially or the right to prevent others from exploiting it are the real issues that lie behind talk about copyright ownership. Agreeing which partners in the project can exercise which rights resolves the problems of ownership. Copyright in materials developed under the project may be owned by the partnership jointly or by individual members. Provided that the partners can agree on a split of the rights and marketing opportunities, together with arrangements for the proper split of income, then issues of ownership do not arise. Centralized responsibility, however, is often the best way to identify copyright clearance needs and obtain the relevant clearances.

2.1.3 CONTROL

Control of the rights granted to the partners may be exercised centrally, by the project management team, or be devolved so that each member exercises independent control over the rights they have been licensed. Both may be suitable, though centralized control may be unwieldy and can give rise to disagreement. Whichever method is agreed should be built into the covering agreement.

2.2 INFRINGEMENT

Participants in collaborative projects share resources, staff time and development costs. As a consequence they bring equally the possibility of infringing the rights of third parties. One of the benefits of centralized rights assessment and clearance is that, at least in theory, the risk of infringement may be reduced by adopting a coordinated approach. The chances of infringement in multimedia collaboration may be greater than for similar single-medium projects. Multimedia collaboration often involves an increased number of participants, bringing together rights cultures across a number of media.

2.3 TERMINATION

The collaborating partners should, at the time of negotiating and drafting the project contract, consider the question of what happens to rights and licences on termination of the contract, or in the event of partners withdrawing before completion. It is standard practice in many agreements for licences to terminate but this can sometimes have the effect of encouraging partners to think twice before committing to an expensive development programmme with no guarantee of being able to exploit rights after termination. For some projects, it may be better to plan in advance an agreed rights split that will become effective on termination and to build that into the project agreement. Different forms of intellectual property may be treated separately in such arrangements. Trade mark licensing, for example, should be considered under advice from a trade mark agent or lawyer specializing in that area.

2.4 GOVERNMENT CONTRACTS

In new areas of development, such as multimedia, it is common for governmental or charitable foundations to fund research and development projects under grant or cost-recovery funding agreements. These often work under standard contractual arrangements developed to cater for a raft of activities across the institution's range. They often seek to acquire copyright in materials developed under the project and retain the right for the sponsoring or funding body to exploit the materials for any of their purposes throughout the duration of copyright. This may make sense in developing text-based materials or in commissioning material entirely developed and created from scratch, but the rights implications make them unsuitable for use in multimedia projects.

The question of ownership of copyright may be handled easily enough, provided that the project developers negotiate the retention of exploitation rights appropriate to their own development plans. However, contracts which specify that materials must be available for all purposes carry an obligation for projects to clear third party materials to that standard. In many cases this will be extremely difficult or impossible. Rights holders will generally refuse to license their material to such an extent. If they do, clearance fees will rise correspondingly, so the use of standard funding contracts has a clear effect on production costs. In practice, the use of standard contract clauses of this kind is done with little thought about the real needs of the project. Small projects aimed at developing new techniques or exploring the medium for teaching, or for reaching a small community audience, do not really need to be cleared for world rights across all media. This should be explored before signing, otherwise project partners will face either higher than necessary clearance costs or taking deliberate action to clear to a lower extent than the contract demands. The problem is particularly common in EU or government funded projects, where contracts often seem to have been drafted with the supply of goods in mind rather than the development of a multimedia production. Addressed as part of the drafting process, the sponsor's rights requirements are often easily tailored to meet those of the project.

Multimedia 3

Multimedia is generally thought of as being the seamless and interactive integration of words, sounds and images. It is different from multiple media, in which the constituent parts normally remain separate, though they may be played or accessed simultaneously. In some comparatively crude forms, multimedia has been in common use for a number of years now and rights acquisitions and clearance departments in many industries clear rights across a number of media as a matter of course. Educational packs come in cardboard boxes which rattle when shaken. They can contain textbooks, videos and audio cassettes, postcards and software and amount to a technologically crude form of multimedia. Television programmes, feature films and other audiovisual productions combine the visual, written and audio media without comment. What is it, then, that turns multimedia into 'multimedia'? Just what is 'multimedia'?

The term is widely used but many definitions fall down by referring too specifically to existing technology rather than to the characteristics of what it can achieve, in the way that early cars, being made in the image of the previously existing technology, more closely resemble horse-drawn carriages than modern cars.

Most common definitions stretch from CD-ROM and CD-I (highly interactive systems) across networked computer-based systems to home entertainment applications such as video on demand and computer games. All take the approach of defining the medium by expressing the specifics of particular hardware platforms.

In a rights environment, defining the system too closely may result in clearance quickly going out of date, left behind by changing technology or by new opportunities for exploitation via another platform. If the clearance is defined only as CD-I, for example, then rights have not been cleared for CD-ROM or for playing through networked systems.

This chapter concentrates upon defining rights by examining the characteristics of the multimedia environment. Multimedia in whichever form is a digital, electronic medium. From this, all things follow.

Digital systems reduce all component parts to a series of binary codes – strings of zeros and ones – which allow the production and its contents to be copied, distributed and edited easily and simply. The most important characteristics are:

- multiple copying without degrading quality;
- digital compression giving enormous capacity;
- distribution and access over long distances and across media without degradation;
- easy manipulation, editing, merging and transfer of images, sound and text.

It is important to take account of these characteristics when clearing for multimedia productions. This allows for the possibility of constructing clearance to take account of future technological advances and not be limited to specific, existing opportunities. It also acknowledges a contradiction that lies at the heart of clearing rights in a multimedia environment: that by challenging a rights holder's ability to control absolutely the exploitation of the work, the characteristics which make the medium so attractive to producers and users simultaneously cause concern for many rights holders. Multimedia – particularly interactive multimedia – passes control of the work into the hands of the user. Income generation, the control of territorial distribution and the protection of the work's integrity (the moral rights of the author) are all essential to the rights holder's position, an informed understanding of which is essential in negotiating clearance. Besides, once production is complete, producers are in the same position as any other rights holder. Concerns about multimedia's potential for loss of control then become universal.

3.1 RIGHTS CLEARANCE STRATEGIES IN PRODUCTION

Knowing the concerns of many rights holders and the sophisticated rights clearance chains that have to be followed in clearing multimedia material, the first lesson to be learned is that an early and full dialogue between the programme maker and those clearing the rights must be set up and maintained. In any production, leaving rights clearance until post-production places the negotiator in a weak position. In multimedia the loss of a section (through denial of or the expense of rights clearance) can be disastrous because of the way in which themed sections of the production interrelate. Apparently unimportant or short pieces of material may act as crossroads for wrap-around or interrelating materials, each focusing on or linking through the same section. If clearance for that section fails late in production, the knock-on effects may well be greater than the plain loss of one item. It may involve a complicated rewrite of the surrounding materials or restructuring the hypertext software links which organize the logic between component parts of the production. This is expensive in terms of production and authoring costs and is likely to delay release of the product. Negotiating under such pressure is not easy once the negotiator's ability to say no is compromised. Without that sanction, reaching an acceptable price is difficult. The temptation is always to accept terms at almost any price in order to get the show on the road.

Timing rights clearance is, therefore, extremely important. It involves a compromise between clearing as early in production as possible (pre-production best of all) and waiting until the contents have been finalized. It can be difficult to clear without knowing the programme contents. (Will it use 20 seconds of music or 90 seconds?) Yet leaving clearance to the last minute, when production is complete, obviously carries penalties. To resolve this tension, contact with rights holders should be made before or early in production to talk through at least 'in principle' clearances. This will allow the producer to select material knowing that rights are available and are within the programme budget, even if prices only become fixed in editing. If the quoted price is too high for the production budget, then negotiate. The clearance process should not be limited to a once-only contact with rights holders. Wherever possible, set up a constructive dialogue with rights holders. They will be keen to see your production succeed. Rights holders profit by licensing rights in the materials they control. In most cases it is to your mutual advantage for the material to be cleared.

Remember, the price may be reasonable in respect of the material on offer but if the budget cannot stretch to cover it, or if paying for one clearance leaves it short for another perhaps more important but less glamorous clearance, then it is too expensive. If a family buys a Mercedes Benz for the school run, there is no point in their trying to negotiate an educational discount. Even if it will only be used to take and collect children from school, the vehicle itself remains a premium product and carries a high value. No amount of negotiating will make it a sensible buy on a limited budget. If the family goes ahead and buys it, what other less glamorous parts of their life will suffer as a result? Will their lifestyle be enhanced sufficiently to make up for financial restrictions imposed elsewhere? Similar questions apply to clearing rights in production. You must retain every chance to say no.

In the main, acquisition strategies evolve depending on whether you are creating a multimedia product from scratch, basing it upon existing material or creating it in conjunction with a tied product in another medium.

3.2 MULTIMEDIA PRODUCTION FROM SPECIALLY COMMISSIONED MATERIAL

Given the opportunity to create a multimedia product using entirely commissioned material, most of the main developers in the industry opt wherever possible to retain complete control of the exploitation rights in the product. Absolute control over rights in the end product can only be achieved by maintaining complete control of rights in acquisition. Given the problems of acquiring and controlling rights in existing materials, the preferred option is to commission new material or create in-house wherever possible. While this has cost implications, it does benefit the producer in several ways:

- It offers complete control.
- Commissioned material can be tailored to match your specifications.
- The issue of authors' moral rights can be addressed.
- Costs may be equal to or lower than rights clearance.

Commissioning material or creating it in-house is the approach most favoured by games producers, for example, and other producers of digital products not based upon existing third party or archive material. Games producers commonly have in-house music workshops as well as software designers and developmental testers. Similarly, a CD-I or CD-ROM producer wishing to illustrate musical instruments in an encyclopaedia would prefer to use a short commissioned recording rather than a commercial recording of an international star. It depends on what is appropriate in the context. Does the producer wish to illustrate the characteristics of the instrument or analyse the interpretation given by the star?

In commissioning materials for multimedia, as for all commissioned material, there is a clear need to start with the notion that ownership of copyright is quite distinct from ownership of a physical object. It is the practice in some industries (notably in public relations) for work – particularly photographic work – to be commissioned by word of mouth without a follow-up written contract. A complete assignment of copyright can only be granted in writing. Work commissioned without contract, or under a contract which takes no account of the assignment of intellectual property rights, remains the copyright of the author. The commissioning agent may own the physical work in the form of artwork, photograph or printed text, but is unable to copy or distribute the material without licence. At its most destructive, such an arrangement could result in the commissioned work being fully incorporated into the production before the author, as copyright holder, asserts rights under copyright. If the production has gone to market the damage could be more severe.

Wherever possible the commissioning producer should seek a complete assignment of copyright and all rights in the nature of copyright for the duration of copyright and any extension thereof. The contract should also specify that the copyright is assigned throughout the world and that it covers reproduction, distribution and sale in any medium either in existence or yet to be invented. Such an assignment allows the producer to use the work without restriction and in any medium. Neither does it restrict use to a particular production. The material is free for use in other productions made under the producer's control and for licensing to other producers. It may involve a complete buy-out of rights (that is, a single once-only payment which acquires all necessary rights without further commitment to pay for future exploitation), in which case no further payment becomes due for subsequent use. Or it may involve the use of stepped payments or royalties which are activated as exploitation develops over time. In that case, although further payment may become due, the producer is assured of the material's availability and can build its cost easily into marketing or development budget calculations.

In choosing either to buy out rights or to use a royalties system, the number of buy-outs and their cost are significant deciding factors. Where rights are not individually significant to the project or may be bought out at comparatively low cost, the buy-out option may be preferable. Known by some as 'blood chits', low fee buy-outs are often used for contributions such as street interviews with members of the public. There was at one time a rule of thumb that said blood chits should be used only for contributions that could end up on the cutting room floor – in other words, for contributions of a comparatively minor or insubstantial nature which could, for reasons as diverse as timing, content or inappropriateness, be cut from the programme without greatly affecting its integrity. That approach has changed and complete assignments or buy-outs are now accepted by many contributors. Other contributions commonly acquired by using buy-outs include still photographs and some music. Talent union agreements covering the use of performers may also make allowance for the buying out of certain rights, although others will invariably be retained for separate negotiation.

In cases where individual rights are significant to the entire project or where a lot of individual buy-outs may amount to a significant proportion of the production budget, a royalty arrangement may be preferred. A royalty of 10% in total of either net income or of the production budget to be made available for splitting among all rights holders is taken by some producers to be a useful guideline in calculating affordable rights costs.

The complete assignment of rights in the work is not always possible. In such cases the contract must specify the rights split which the parties have agreed. The commissioning producer must in such circumstances have a clear view of the production's intended use. This may be broken down for ease of reference into three distinct categories: the prime, core intent of the programme for which obtaining rights is essential; the secondary market for which strong possibilities exist; and wider, long-term possibilities which may become firmer through time.

Rights for the core activities must be acquired early in production. It is administratively easier to acquire them at point of contracting by making additional payments, if necessary. Buy-outs are commonly preferred. Those for secondary and tertiary exploitation may be guaranteed by exercising options, by which rights are assured subject to payment being made (by either royalty or lump sum) at the point of exploitation and not before.

In an environment which depends upon the manipulation of material it is not enough to assume the rights needed for full post-production exploitation will always be available or that copyright clearance is enough. Moral rights may be infringed by the manipulation of material during production. Colourizing, manipulating the image, editing and displacement of materials may all infringe moral rights. Commissioning contracts should ask for moral rights to be waived wherever possible under UK legislation. Moral rights are inalienable in continental Europe, however, and waivers made under UK law only hold good for products distributed in the UK. Once distribution takes place in other EU member states, moral rights may be enforced. To take account of this, contracts should specify in advance that the commissioned material is likely to be manipulated. As far as possible, the degree of manipulation should also be specified.

One effect of multimedia is almost certain to be that the benefits of promoting and maintaining a good relationship between producer or publisher and author will become even more valuable. However future rights clauses are drafted in contracts, it is likely that the intent of the contract will be outpaced by technological developments in the way that older music publishing contracts were left behind by developments in CD technology. This means that publishers and producers can be less confident that existing contracts will guarantee future exploitation through technologies as yet to be developed and places a greater reliance upon their developing a closer collaborative relationship with authors and other contributors. An author who is closely involved in the development of an extension to or amendment of the original work, such as in multimedia, will be more willing to co-operate in granting further rights. The impossibility of guaranteeing moral rights waivers outside the UK adds to this. For a fuller examination of moral rights questions, see Chapter 10.

The manipulation of material in production also means that the material must be supplied in an accessible format. This applies particularly to electronic artwork. Should any vagueness in the contract allow that the artwork could be supplied in a read-only format, the commissioning producer will not be able to access and manipulate the material. Access to an interactive format would only be possible with the co-operation of the graphic artist, subject to another contract and another payment.

3.3 USING EXISTING MATERIALS

Producers with a smaller budget or working with factually based projects, such as encyclopaedias, may find it difficult to create an entirely new product from scratch. In that case, third party copyright material will be selected and cleared for use. Third party material is much less under the direct control of the producer. It is unlikely to be available under exclusive licence; it may not be under the control of a single owner and may itself be restricted by complicated and restricted rights clearance covering its own use of third party material. A publisher, for example, with a stable of authors under contract may be unable to license the multimedia rights you require. A significant proportion of those authors are likely to have been contracted many years ago under contracts which made no mention of multimedia or electronic rights. Multimedia rights in their material will not be under control of the publisher. Clearing it for use in your own production will mean contacting each author individually. In order to assess the level of clearance necessary, it is useful to look at a rights audit trail through the multimedia production and distribution process.

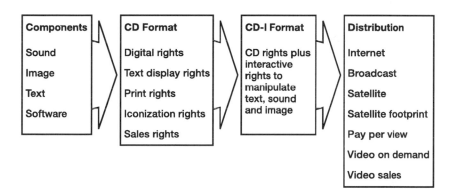

Figure 3.1   Linear development of rights clearance

Figure 3.1 shows the linear development of successive needs for rights clearance from the original selection of source material through the CD formats to delivery. Although the figure is expressed as a form of linear development model, it is not necessarily the case that in order to distribute via the Internet, for instance, all other rights along the figure's horizontal development must also be acquired. It is possible to broadcast by satellite without wishing to broadcast terrestrially, and to distribute via the Net without wishing to manipulate the material. However, Figure 3.1 does illustrate a commonly perceived development in rights from simple to complex. Notice that the CD formats include the clearance of rights to display lyrics and other text on screen, to authorize users to print them as hard copy and to represent pictorial images as icons in screen displays.

3.3.1 THIRD PARTY TEXT

At some point in the production of material in almost any medium, the author's work is expressed in written form. Television and film productions move through a scripted stage before filming, animated programmes have story boards, music and lyrics are often written or sketched out before performance. Text is a useful starting point in examining the rights challenges presented by the new and emerging technologies.

Multimedia and other forms of electronic delivery systems represent a huge change to established publishing practices, more so probably than to any other media industry. The result is that publishers may seem slow to move towards establishing new industry practices to replace the old. This can be frustrating to those producers coming from other industries who have already been through the process of change, to whom print publishers may seem slow and hesitant in their response. There are constraints, however, that restrict publishers' freedom of response. Many established print contracts were drawn up some years ago and are unlikely to cover the type of exploitation now demanded by multimedia producers and audiences. Re-clearing an entire back catalogue is a time-consuming and expensive business, yet without going through that exercise publishers cannot be certain of controlling the rights they are granting. The process of re-clearance is one which is confronted by many other industries, such as film and television, but is a particular problem for publishing – an industry which is having to face the clearing of rights in ways alien to most of its history. It is important to bear this in mind when approaching publishers. No consistent industry response has yet been established. In the absence of one, it is dangerous to assume that permission will be forthcoming, though permission for quotation rights in a printed medium might have been.

This results in inconsistent pricing policies between publishers. Some are reserving multimedia and electronic rights completely while others are assessing each request on its merits. Where publishers are willing to grant reproduction rights, the going rate appears to fall approximately within a range equivalent to 100% and 200% of print reproduction rates in the world (English language) market. Thus material which would cost, say, £100 to clear for English language rights in the world market would cost between £100 and £200 to clear for multimedia use. The territory may also be restricted to the UK or European Union rather than throughout the world.

This range of pricing is much wider than one would expect for equivalent print rights, where publishers generally have evolved pricing policies that vary remarkably little between houses.

It also only covers use on CD-ROM. If you intend to authorize users to print hard copy from the CD-ROM, then print rights will be required. (The concept of authorization is an important one and must be explicitly avoided unless you are certain that you control the rights you are authorizing others to use.)

3.3.2 BACK CATALOGUE MATERIALS

Established producers or publishers will come to multimedia projects with an already existing back catalogue of material. The feeling, particularly among those with a limited understanding of intellectual property, is often that control of the back catalogue in book or programme form represents a continuing control that extends into the newer media such as CD-ROM or CD-I. This is not the case. In fact, it is more likely than not that the ability to control back catalogue material will be tied up under older contracts which make no provision for exploitation in the electronic or digital formats. The problem was faced by the television companies when they sought to release materials for exploitation on commercial satellite channels, for release on CD formats and for the re-packaging of classic series several years after their initial success. The repeat of classic series such as *Elizabeth R* may be delayed for a considerable time while repeat fees are negotiated and the entire cast of the original series contacted for their agreement. It is a vast, time-consuming and expensive process and cannot be avoided. Repeat fees alone for a classic series may run into hundreds of thousands of pounds. How much more difficult it is to clear an entire back catalogue for exploitation in new formats, particulary when the information storage capacity of the new formats is so great that individual clearances regularly run into thousands.

To some extent the broadcasting industry has several advantages when negotiating the extension of existing clearances to cover electronic formats. Existing contracts in an industry dependent upon technological delivery systems may already define some formats so widely that, in effect, CD format rights have already been granted. In some contracts, for example, videogram rights may be defined as 'videocassettes, videodiscs and any other device for reproducing visual images and sound which may be played back by the use of a playback device'.

While the term 'videogram' may now seem a little dated, it is useful to see how a somewhat out-of-date expression may yet remain relevant by virtue of its definition as it is expressed in the contract. It is how the term is defined, rather than the term itself, that carries clout.

In addition, in an industry where collective agreements negotiated by talent unions on behalf of their members are common practice, it is possible for producers and broadcasters to negotiate and amend contracts to cover evolving rights requirements in a single negotiation binding on talent union members. Standard existing agreements may also be amended in this way as part of an updating process which may, in certain circumstances, be held to alter contracts already in place.

The question remains, however, one of whether or nor contracts willingly entered into at one point of technological development can be said to hold good in times of rapidly evolving formats, each of which may require additional and exceptional rights clearance. Even all-rights contracts specifying that the contribution may be used for all purposes in all formats, in existence now or yet to be developed, might not in some circumstances provide adequate coverage for future projects. The contract rests upon the parties' understanding of its meaning at the time of signing. It could be argued that a particular format developed at some point in the future represents such an enormous leap forward in the potential to exploit the material that it could not reasonably be considered to fall under the intention of the contract. If a format does not yet exist, can it be held that there was indeed any intention to license its use?

A case involving the Disney corporation centred around a similar debate when it was argued by the rights owners of the musical sound recording used in the film *Fantasia* that Disney's right to exploit the film did not extend to release on video. Such arguments were also met by the recording industry when CD recordings of analogue back catalogue material were first released.

A possible rule of thumb might be to follow the example of television broadcasters and use all-rights contracts for material which can be 'left on the cutting room floor' (material which may be dropped from the programme without affecting its value). The relative importance of the contribution to the work as a whole is a useful guide to what rights a reasonable producer and contributor might expect to be covered by an all-rights contract.

The confusion over what rights may be assumed without extending existing contracts combines with authors' rights under moral rights provisions in the UK and, more importantly, in continental Europe to place a premium upon publishers and producers building and maintaining good working relationships with their authors. As the media move towards the electronic transfer of rights and away from the sale of physical objects (books, CDs, cassettes, etc.), so the role of the publisher/producer moves correspondingly closer to that of an agent. They become less involved in the production of physical objects and more concerned with the exploitation through licensing of their intangible rights of exploitation in work produced by a stable of talent. In such a situation authors may become more intimately involved in the subsequent use of their work in other formats, through consultation and agreement rather than by force of contract.

3.4 CD-ROM FORMAT

The CD-ROM is a patented format developed by Philips and licensed exclusively by them. Use of the format and the CD symbol is granted under licence. CD-ROM products must conform to the hardware and software standards laid down in the *Red Book*, which is available from Philips in either hard copy or on disk.

It is sometimes assumed that the term 'CD' is a generic title for all interactive and digital formats and poorly drafted licences may make use of the term loosely. In fact specifying CD-ROM rights will exclude CD-I, networked computer systems and other digital formats which might yet come on line. It refers specifically to the right to include material in the CD-ROM platform.

The term also stops short of specifying exactly what rights are required by a particular project. Including material on a CD is one thing, but how is the material to be manipulated or displayed as part of the normal use of the product?

To take a piece of music, for example, it is possible to play the music as a sound recording, to accompany the audio track with a visual display of the song lyrics and to permit the user to print the lyrics as hard copy. Each of these uses represents a different level of rights clearance not covered by the term CD-ROM.

The producer might also wish to authorize users to mount the CD on a networked computer system. That, too, requires additional license. Will the CD be accessed by remote users? How will access be made? How will it be licensed: via site licences or local area networks, or per user or per platform? All are possible and the rights owner licensing the use of third party material for use in a CD-ROM production will require full details before the licence is drafted. (Chapter 9 refers to software and networked rights in detail.)

Above all, the producer must remain constantly aware that the product under development can only be licensed to the extent that licences in third party material have been obtained. Users of the finished product cannot be authorized to commit acts which may infringe the rights of other rights holders. In the development of double cassette audio recorders, for example, the music industry strongly objected to advertisements promoting a particular product because, it was claimed, they encouraged users to make copy recordings from original music cassettes, so damaging trade and infringing the rights of owners in the original recordings. The case turned upon whether or not the manufacturer of the cassette recorder was held to have licensed and authorized infringement by users of the product or merely to have explained what was possible. In the event, it was held that the manufacturers did not cross beyond the threshold of advertising the capabilities of the system they had developed and were promoting. They did not authorize infringement.

Similar considerations must arise when examining the mounting of CDs on networked systems. Producers cannot authorize or licence the use of products beyond the level of copyright clearance that they have secured in the course of production. It may be possible for users to network the content of a CD or to manipulate or edit its contents but the producer can only authorize the use of the CD for those purposes if the appropriate third party rights have been secured.

3.5 CD-I FORMAT

Like CD-ROM, CD-I is a patented system which must be used under licence. In this case CD-I products must conform to the hardware and software standards laid down by the *Green Book*, which is available from Philips in hard copy or on disk. Producers must comply with its standards before a licence to use the trademark is granted, in much the same way that sound recordings must meet a technical threshold before being able to use the Dolby butterfly trade mark.

All rights necessary for CD-ROM use must also be cleared for use on CD-I but with the notable addition of interactive rights. These are considered and licensed separately by many rights owners.

They also interact strongly with the author's right to protect the moral rights in the work. For CD-I in particular it is essential for producers to come to an understanding with authors regarding moral rights, for the medium stands or falls on its ability to allow for the manipulation of material by the end user as well as the producer. This means that authors (not just the rights holders) must be aware of the ways that their material may possibly be manipulated. It calls for close involvement of the authors in the production process.

Even in instances where the contents of a CD-I disk have been created entirely under the control of the producer or with the direct supervision of the artist (for example, in the development of a CD-I disk promoting a rock performer's recent release), the subsequent licensing of the disk should rarely include the right of users to use their manipulated version of the disk for anything other than personal, home use. In the case of some CD-I disks, for example, it is possible for users to re-mix the music track to create an entirely new balance between the instruments. This use was licensed for home, personal use only, otherwise the artist's own ability to exploit the work would have been damaged by the probable release of alternative mix versions of the original recording.

3.6 THE INTERNET

The Internet and other international systems of interacting communication between computer-based access points, such as Super Janet in the UK and World Wide Web, present challenges to commercial producers of copyright.

The dominant ethos of the Internet has grown from two sources, both of which are at odds with the commercial exploitation of intellectual property rights and sit uneasily with evolving access to the Internet by commercial users. The first of these is the prevailing view of early developers and users of the Internet that information should be a freely available and shared resource; the second is that the Internet developed with an extremely high proportion of users coming from the academic community, which already has an ethos of sharing information and research.

As a consequence, commercial exploitation and the protection of intellectual property rights are uncomfortable within the currently prevailing ethos of the Net. This causes producers and publishers to be wary when licensing material for use on the Net and when considering their own options for using it – publishing electronic journals, for example. It also means that a high proportion of users, though mostly well-intentioned, may be at repeated risk of infringing copyright through ignorance. Copyright notices attached to access sites, say, may be wrongly interpreted by some users as releasing material rather than restricting access. Other users creating bulletin boards may infringe the rights of those whose material they publish and a number of access sites have closed as a result of rights infringements involving the use of bulletin boards to post information on Elvis Presley and other celebrity figures. Yet the Rolling Stones have also used the Internet to provide a live relay of a concert and a recent video by Madonna was available for some time for users to download extremely slowly over a period of about a week.

The informal tenor of communications on the Net also promotes a dangerously comfortable sense of being among friends in the senior common room. Unfortunately conversations among friends can run a considerable risk of attracting action for libel when accessed by an audience of thousands across the Net, though it may be difficult for plaintiffs to take action outside their own judiciary.

The other difficulties are those of ring-fencing to limit access or territorial distribution, and that of coding or marking material in order to be able to track its use across the system.

The difficulty of restricting distribution may best be dealt with by licensors simply assuming that material may be accessed in an unrestricted way and charging accordingly.

The issue of coding material, branding it in some way like cattle released to roam free on the range, is more difficult because it confronts the issue of piracy. Technological solutions have been proposed and are constantly under development but they share a common weakness in that, at some point in its life, material must be released for access by legitimate users. At that point all systems become vulnerable. If technology can encode, then reverse technology can decode – as US satellite broadcasters are finding to their cost when business worth approximately half a billion dollars per year is lost through sales of decoders based upon pirated chip technology.

Having first failed with technological solutions, the computer software industry confronted the issue by reducing prices until consumers felt it was fair to pay licence fees rather than use unlicensed copies on their machines. The same option may yet prove effective for material accessed by the developing networked systems.

Meanwhile automatic digital auditing and tracking systems are being developed to monitor networked access to electronic journals, etc. and to levy fees for access which are then distributed to rights holders, though the task of tracking and auditing millions of small payments back from users to publishers' and authors' collecting societies is enormous. Such development projects, recognizing that absolute copyright protection is almost certainly impossible, are concentrating upon making it cheaper and easier for users to behave legitimately by paying copyright fees than illegitimately. Projects share several characteristics and typically would allow for materials to be accessed and supplied in an encrypted, unreadable form via the Internet. They could only be decrypted using an electronic coding available from the rights holder or a trusted third party, such as a collecting society. The coding would be capable of releasing different levels of access (read-only; printed copy for personal use; republication by a publisher) and is specific to the user, the material and the access machine. Fees set according to level of access would be routed back to rights holders.

3.6.1 MATERIAL DEVELOPED ON THE INTERNET

Internet users sometimes distinguish between material developed in the course of networked conversations displayed on bulletin boards and other commercially or privately produced materials developed outside the Net. There is an assumption that messages posted to a bulletin board may be used freely for any purpose by other accessed users of the board. This is not so. The status of letters posted to the board is similar in some respects to that of letters posted to a newspaper's letters column, in that there is an implied licence to publish in the columns of the newspaper but not to publish elsewhere, either by the newspaper or by its readers. Copyright in individual postings on the Internet is retained by the author. Any implied licence to copy to other users of the bulletin board does not extend to downloading the material for use or publication elsewhere either in print or in other formats. Users contributing to the development materials using the Internet as a means of communication should also be aware that the collaborative nature of this kind of writing means that it can be difficult to untangle the ownership of copyright in the finished product. Indeed there is a real sense in which collaboration of this kind may never stop, and there evolves a collective responsibility for the creation of the work. It is wise to treat this like other collaborative developments and agree the ownership and licensing of copyright among the partners before work starts.

3.7 INTERACTIVE RIGHTS

One of the characteristics of digital media is the ability for producers to create games or stories combining live and animated action with a number of possible narrative structures selected by users in the course of play. Publishers may be familiar with a comparatively unwieldy print version of this fantasy/game-playing format which allows the reader to make creative storyline decisions at various points in the text by choosing to rejoin the narrative at another page. For multimedia producers the combination of live and animated sequences allows players to decide, for instance, whether or not to slay the dragon or to attempt to make it an ally. According to that decision, the narrative is altered so as to present the player with differing challenges or other options in the narrative. In production, this alters the performances of live actors. Having to perform a series of sequences as alternatives to the central narrative thread means that actors will be required to perform a greater number of scenes than they would otherwise play in a conventionally structured production.

In May 1995 Equity signed the first of its agreements covering the terms and fee structure relating to its members performing in an interactive production. Producers seeking to engage actors for an interactive production of this kind should contact Equity or other relevant performers' bodies to negotiate an agreement in advance of production. In such circumstances a union's ability to act on behalf of its members can prove to be equally useful to producers in working out a collective agreement to cover the engagement of all union members performing in the production. Having such an agreement in place will make it easier to engage performers, particularly when the working format may be comparatively novel and untested.

Text **4**

Written or printed material either taken from other works or specially commissioned for your project are protected by copyright as literary or dramatic works as soon as they are recorded in a material form. The form could be written, or in a sound or video recording of the work or on a record, disc or computer disk containing the work. Copyright protection does not extend to the work until fixation, so a verbal briefing of a commissioned author does not qualify for protection. There are differences in the ways in which authors or rights holders should be approached for permission to use their work, depending upon the category of material you wish to use.

4.1 FREE USE

The first question asked by most users of third party material is: what can be used without payment, without permission? The answer is defined by individual circumstances but a routine checklist will allow for most cases to be assessed accurately and with confidence.

4.1.1 OUT-OF-COPYRIGHT MATERIAL

Under EU harmonization legislation effective from 1 July 1995, copyright protection lasts for a period of 70 years after the year in which the author dies. If the material you wish to use falls outside the 70-year limit, copyright will have expired and the material may be used freely.

A revised edition of the work may have been produced more recently and that will have attracted copyright protection as a work in its own right. Similar care must be exercised in quoting from modern editions of classic texts, for example, where new commentaries may have been added, together with footnotes and other expositional material. Quoting the new edition in its entirety – footnotes, glossary of terms *et al.* – will infringe copyright unless clearance is obtained. The complication is more likely to arise in cases where texts are scanned into computer programs or used as camera-ready copy for conventional print editions. The physical reproduction of existing works in any event carries an additional protection offered to the publisher's copyright in the typographical arrangement of the text, a protection offered for a period of 25 years after publication. Finding material entirely free of copyright protection can be more difficult than it seems.

Even the use of government material placed in the public domain, and often seen as a good source of unrestricted material, can carry production costs that are often overlooked. All US government material is placed in the public domain and is available without copyright cost. However, just as film researchers may find that the process of obtaining the physical print of the film may carry high laboratory and travel costs, so, too, may those seeking to use, for example, NASA images of space, find that they carry origination or access costs that are important not to overlook.

4.1.2 FREE USE ALLOWED UNDER THE COPYRIGHT, DESIGNS AND PATENTS ACT 1988

The system of protection offered under copyright depends to a large extent for its success on participants relying upon the fair treatment of their work within the framework offered by statutory protection. It could be extremely easy to use material without permission or due payment, but then the system would fail, to the detriment of all. If an impecunious student with a large pocket hidden in an overcoat shoplifts books needed for the course, it is unlikely that they will be caught. Does that mean that shoplifting is acceptable in the circumstances? Would the argument that they were stealing for 'educational purposes' be an adequate defence?

In any dealing with third party material the first questions to be asked are:

- Is the use fair?
- Will it harm the rights owner's ability to exploit the work elsewhere?
- Are you using the most important or significant part of the original?

The answers to these three questions will provide guidance on whether or not the material may be used without clearance and also indicate the rights holder's likely response if clearance is needed: will they agree your request and, if so, how much might they be likely to charge?

4.1.3 FAIR DEALING

The 1988 Copyright Act makes provision for the quoting of material from a copyright work with the allowance of 'fair dealing ... for the purposes of criticism or review', provided that sufficient acknowledgement is made to the author and the work. It applies as a defence in cases where, in normal circumstances, copyright would clearly have been infringed by the quoting of a substantial part of a copyright work. The defence hinges about its middle, so that in order to qualify for your use to be considered fair dealing for the purposes of criticism or review, use of the work must be fair and must also be for the purposes of bona fide criticism or review. The quote may be used to illustrate a review of the original from which it is taken, or to illuminate criticism of another work. Nowhere does the Act define a maximum quotation beyond which this allowance does not apply.

In practice, criticism and review have been interpreted to be close to what is generally understood to be the business of a critic or reviewer – for example, a review of a play or film or the literary review of a book. They have been taken to exclude most typical educational material, where the function is pedagogical rather than critical.

The second part of the defence which turns about its hinge is the question of whether or not the use of the material is 'fair'. Again, the Act does not specify by length or quantity; it simply states that the concept of fairness must apply. In practice, this has been taken to mean that sufficient material may be quoted for the purposes of the act of criticizing or reviewing, and not more. An excellent illustration (though in a different medium) of the way in which 'fair dealing' may be used as a defence against allegations of infringement centred on the use of footage from the film *A Clockwork Orange* in a television review programme. The film had long been withdrawn by its producer, Stanley Kubrick, from screenings in the UK and he had successfully protected his rights in the film by taking action for infringement against a cinema which had screened the film in London. In the case of the television programme, the broadcasters successfully argued that the use of over 10 minutes of footage taken from the film was essential to the programme's ability to criticize or review the work. Though the footage was a substantial part of the film, it was accepted that the use made of *A Clockwork Orange* in the programme was 'fair dealing for the purposes of criticism or review'.

4.1.4 REPORTING CURRENT EVENTS

Material may be quoted freely for the purposes of reporting current events, again subject to sufficient acknowledgement being made to the author and the work. The exception to this defence is that photographs may not be used without permission. The allowance and exception is an interesting illustration of the ways in which copyright legislation interacts with an expression of the public interest and successful industry lobbying. The news media have always fought hard to defend their right to quote material from copyright works in newspapers, on television or on radio. The practicalities of having to clear material day after day to meet extremely short deadlines would make it impossible to avoid infringement. Free use in this context means that news reporting can retain its immediacy and that copyright cannot be used as a means of inhibiting reporting. The public interest, in this instance, is taken to override the apparent interests of publishers and authors. On the other hand, the interests of the press photographic agencies have been recognized by placing the unauthorized use of their work outside this provision.

A useful illustration of the amount of leeway given under this provision by the judiciary concerns the use by one broadcaster of a rival's exclusive transmission from the 1990 World Cup. By successfully arguing that they were reporting current events, the broadcaster was able to transmit goals and other significant action from the matches as part of their news and current affairs output.

Newspaper 'spoiler' stories (stories run in competition with a rival paper's exclusive) operate along similar lines by using quotes taken from the rival's previous edition to produce a competing spoiler.

It is clear, however, that this form of free use applies strictly to the reporting of current events. Unless the material is for immediate use, such as a documentary of current events, the defence may be of little value.

4.1.5 FREE USE OF AN 'INSUBSTANTIAL PART'

If the use of a 'substantial' part of a copyright work without permission constitutes infringement, then it follows that use of an 'insubstantial' part of a work would not constitute infringement. The Act does not define either 'substantial' or 'insubstantial'. For an answer to that, legal precedent is the only guide, though some industry guidelines have evolved for the benefit of those involved in the publishing industries. The Publishers Association guidelines suggest that an insubstantial part of a long work, such as a novel or an extended journal article, may be taken to be up to 400 words of continuous prose or 800 words of discontinuous text, provided that no single extract exceeds 300 words. For shorter works, such as shorter newspaper or journal articles, the guidelines suggest that the quote should not exceed 10% of the original.

Two things have to be stressed, though: that the guidelines are no more than guidelines and that they use a relatively simple equation which considers substantiality in terms of length. Precedence suggests strongly that substantiality has much more to do with significance or importance than with volume. It is a qualitative rather than a quantitative judgement. Quoting from a murder mystery the sentence which gives away the nub of the plot may be an infringement of copyright – the sentence may be considered a substantial part of the work as a whole, the denouement of the plot resting upon it. Yet a much longer extract from another work may not be considered to be a substantial part and hence not an infringement.

Poetry, sheet music and lyrics all illustrate the degree to which notions of substantiality rely upon interpreting the significance of the part to the whole.

4.1.6 POETRY

It is extremely difficult to quote any section of poetry without the quote being substantial, not because of the ratio between the quotation and the (generally short) whole poem, but because there is little in a poem that can be considered insubstantial. Every word has to fight for its space in the line. One well known case against infringement was brought against the makers of the tonic wine Sanatogen for their use in an advertisement of four lines from the Kipling poem 'If'. There was no dispute that the work was in copyright. Sanatogen's defence rested upon the fact that only four lines were quoted and that they were not sufficient to constitute a significant part of the poem. Sanatogen was found to have infringed copyright.

4.1.7 SHEET MUSIC AND LYRICS

Like poetry, music and song lyrics are both included in the provision of fair dealing for the purposes of criticism and review and for the reporting of current events. Like poetry, they are both treated as being particularly difficult to quote without making use of a substantial part of the work. The precedent to consider here involved the use of eight notes from the song 'Over the Rainbow' by Arlen and Harburg (a song, incidentally, which originally was so lacking in significance that it was almost dropped from *The Wizard of Oz*). In view of this and given the contestants' ability in a popular game to name the tune quickly from only a couple of notes, it is difficult to imagine any use of a copyright musical work which does not involve a significant part – something which has increased in importance with the rapid growth of electronically sampled drum beats, guitar parts, etc. taken from one recording and used in another. This is done legally under licence from the Mechanical Copyright Protection Society (MCPS), the producer having taken advice from the Music Publishers Association.

4.1.8 TABLES, GRAPHS AND OTHER ILLUSTRATIONS

Tables, graphs and other illustrations, and individual entries in reference works such as encyclopaedias and dictionaries, are entire works in their own right. They enjoy copyright protection separate from the protection given to the parent work from which they come (see also Chapter 5).

Each self-contained work of this kind, such as a table showing house prices in the UK and its regions, or a graph showing their fluctuations for the post-war years, is protected separately by copyright. The provisions for use under the various defences offered by the Act apply. Short extracts constituting an insubstantial part of the whole may be quoted without infringing.

It is very important to remember that the protection offered by copyright is granted to the expression of the idea or information, and not to the information itself. This sometimes seems unfair and, therefore, may be confusing. Nevertheless, it remains a fact that the information expressed within a table or graph may be used freely, without infringement, if it is expressed in an entirely new format which makes no use of the original expression. Good practice still requires, though, that the original source is cited clearly. On a practical level, as well as being good academic practice, it may also provide protection against unwarranted accusations of plagiarism or passing off. Avoiding such accusations and the difficulties they bring are as significant as avoiding the infringement of copyright.

For illustrations, the same rules apply but it may prove to be more difficult to re-draw the illustration and retain the sense of it while dropping any significant trace of the original expression. For example, a cartoonist enjoys the benefit of copyright protection in the drawing but not in the joke it contains. It is possible to create a completely new drawing telling the same joke, avoiding the need to obtain copyright clearance before publication, but it could be that seeking clearance is the easier option.

4.2 PERFORMANCE OR ADAPTATION

The performance of an existing play or the adaptation of a novel into a dramatized form requires the approval of the copyright owner. The right to perform a copyright work is a restricted act, as are the rights to adapt the work or to broadcast it. Making use of a copyright work, even if it is not in the form of a direct copy, will require clearance.

When a broadcaster plans the production of a dramatized play or series based upon an existing copyright work, their first step is to clear the adaptation or dramatization rights with the author or rights holder of the work to be adapted. In practice these rights are normally assigned by authors to their publishers. Once the adaptation rights have been cleared, the adaptation itself (a new copyright work in its own right) is commissioned. Copyrights in the two works co-exist. Should at any time a new adaptation be commissioned, based not on the original novel but on the adaptation, the rights holders of both the original and the adaptation would have to permit the subsequent version. This could arise, for instance, in the case of a modern novel adapted for broadcast as a television series or serial and subsequently adapted for release as a Hollywood movie.

Even though copyright and other rights will have been cleared prior to production, the author retains the right to object to derogatory treatment of the work under the right of integrity introduced to UK copyright legislation under the 1988 Act (Chapter 10). In effect, the author maintains a need to be consulted on any adaptation of the work in order for the broadcaster to be assured that the adaptation is not derogatory.

Rights granted and acquired in the commissioning contract will give the broadcaster the right to contract the adaptation and to produce and transmit the final programme or series. Without those, the broadcaster would have the right to adapt but no right to transmit the subsequent piece of work.

4.3 CLEARANCE PROCESS

The first step in the clearance process must always be identifying and contacting the rights holder. This might not necessarily be the author.

A simple starting point is the publisher. The publisher normally handles the clearance of extract rights, either on behalf of the author or as owner of the rights itself, having bought them out as part of the original publishing contract.

It is essential to save time by approaching the original publisher as quickly as possible, rather than approach the publisher of a recent edition or of a text in which the original material appears merely as an extract. The acknowledgements page or the copyright line in the book must always be the starting point. Check whether the material is credited to another source or whether the entire book, as may be the case, is reprinted by permission or by arrangement with another publisher. Then approach the source credited.

Specify clearly the rights required – for example, 'World distribution in the English language in print' or 'Distribution throughout Europe in the English and French languages on CD-ROM'. (In the latter example, 'Europe' is different from 'the European Union'.)

Publishers will want to have details of the proposed print run, or the number of users in the case of electronic rights. It is likely that they will also request details of the context in which the work is to be set, so as to ensure that the author is not to be misrepresented in setting up a misleading or confrontational argument – in the case of an academic text, for example. This, and other considerations such as accidentally perpetuating a libel, underline the importance of maintaining good contact with rights holders and their representatives.

Many publishers prefer approaches for permission to use material to be made in writing, in contrast to some other media industries where the telephone, fax or, increasingly, electronic mail is the normal means of communication. Some insist on using their own application and licensing forms. One prominent US academic and business school publisher uses a two-page form requiring details of the precise material to be quoted, the publisher's own reference number, precisely the context in which their material will be used, the name(s) of the author(s) of the proposed work, its proposed print run and the percentage of the new work which will be made up of their licensed material. All this is in addition to further questions relating to cover price, extent and the full name of the clerk processing the application. Filling in such forms can be extremely taxing and time consuming at a time when print deadlines may be pressing.

The clearance process can be a long one. Publishers and other rights holders might take a considerable time to respond to approaches for permission to quote material but this is not always because they have not read the letter. Often only one person deals with permission requests and they, too, are not always free to act without checking the rights ownership of the material and liaising with authors and colleagues as to the extent to which the material is clear to be licensed.

Publishers may not be in control of the rights requested: they may have to refer to the author or an agent; they may control only some of the rights requested or only some of the territories in which they are to be exercised. Publishers can only licence to the extent to which they in turn control rights in the material.

This is seen most frequently in the division of rights by geographical territory. Clearing the use of material throughout the world often entails clearing rights with separate publishers for certain territorial blocks. This is particularly the case for the US, its territories and its dependencies. It is a commonplace for a UK publisher to control rights in Europe and elsewhere, with the exception of US rights – generally held by a US publisher or US subsidiary.

4.3.1 DEFINING RIGHTS

It is important to be clear about the rights required for each individual project. Material may be requested for use in an article to be published in a low-circulation academic journal, or in translation or for performance. The permutations can seem endless and allow for expensive conjecture on the part of the rights holder unless proposals are explained clearly.

Unless those seeking clearance of material are familiar with rights conventions within the publishing industry, it may be best to write with a clear prose description of the rights being sought. No one should know the producer's intent better than the producer and a licence or contract is, ultimately, a prose description of an agreement between parties. In a time of cross-media contracting for use of material there is potential for conflicts of misunderstanding between licensees and licensors coming from unfamiliar rights clearance and licensing cultures and conventions. The clearest licences may result from straightforward prose descriptions of projects and their intended markets rather than upon the traditional rights terminology of one industry or another.

Defining rights

When describing the rights required for a specific project the important points to remember are:

1. *What use is being made of the material?*
2. *In what medium is the material being used?*
3. *Over what territory will the material be distributed?*
4. *How will you distribute the material in the territory?*
5. *Over what period of time will the material be distributed?*
6. *How many copies of the material will be distributed?*
7. *What price will be charged for or what income will be earned from the distribution of the product?*

Licences, even in the form of simple letters of approval, must be read carefully to match rights granted against the rights requested, a point so obvious that it is often overlooked, particularly by those relatively inexperienced in the business of clearing rights. Standard contracts, used by many publishers, may not match exactly the particular rights requirements of individual projects. This is particularly true in the case of material being cleared for use in interactive, digital or electronic formats. Many publishers are understandably wary of granting rights in these formats and may not, in any case, be clear about the nature of the rights required. They may initially refuse permission unless the nature of the production can be explained fully. Publishers are particularly in need of reassurance about the nature and extent of protection that multimedia producers can guarantee against unauthorized or unrestricted copying.

Unless restricted access and use can be guaranteed, it is not surprising that rights holders may chose to refuse clearance. They are particularly concerned about the opportunity for abuse offered by dissemination via networks world wide, such as the Internet or World Wide Web, where material may be used without control or restriction and with no record of where it has been downloaded. This takes control away from legitimate rights holders and some see that their only protection lies in refusing permission for any interactive use, at least until the control structures of the new and emerging media become fixed.

4.3.2 CONDITIONS OF PERMISSION

Publishers may set conditions of use in their licence. These may range from specifying the rights granted to the provision of a free copy of the work in which their material will be quoted. Licences must be read with care to check that the licensor has granted all necessary rights and that the licensee is in a position to meet the restrictions imposed on their use. Production being the result of commercial as well as artistic effort, fees requested by publishers must be assessed in terms of the project budget, rather than whether or not they represent good value in themselves. Many publishers work to standard fee structures and are unwilling or unable to negotiate. Others may be more responsive. In any event, it must never be assumed that fees quoted are fixed and without room for manoeuvre. Ultimately the material must come within the producer's available budget or it is too expensive to use.

Checking replies

The following checklist gives a guide to the standard response to any licence:

1. *Is the fee acceptable?*
2. *Have all necessary rights been granted?*
3. *Is the territorial clearance adequate?*
4. *Does another rights holder have to be contacted?*
5. *Are conditions of use acceptable or can they be negotiated?*
6. *Is the complete print run covered?*
7. *Have other language rights been granted?*
8. *Has an acknowledgement line been specified?*
9. *Must a free copy of the work be provided on publication?*
10. *Is the acknowledgement to be placed by the extract or on an acknowledgements page?*

Rights may be limited by duration, by numbers of copies or accessed users, or by other restrictions the rights owner may impose in the licence. Being aware of these imposes a responsibility on producers to be aware of their own position and fix a response.

Will the producer be best served by negotiating at the point of licensing or by accepting conditions as they stand, with the intention of going back to the rights holder at a later date?

Is it possible, actually, for the producer to comply with all the conditions imposed by the licence and still produce an effective or aesthetically pleasing product?

4.4 ACKNOWLEDGEMENTS

Permission to quote is always dependent upon proper acknowledgement, even if the acknowledgement line is not specified in detail. In printed text this is placed either by the quoted item or on a separate acknowledgements page. House styles vary but here are some reasonable acknowledgements:

1. A quote from the book *How to Write Acknowledgements*, by John O'Brien, published in 1994:

   O'Brien, J. (1994) *How to Write Acknowledgements*, Bloggs Publishers Ltd.
2. A quote from the article 'How to write acknowledgements', by John O'Brien, in the journal *Clearing Rights* published on 4 June 1994:

   O'Brien, J. (1994) 'How to write acknowledgements', from *Clearing Rights*, Vol. 4, 4 June 1994.

This form is not necessary for the statutory requirement to acknowledge the source of material used under the provisions of fair dealing (sections 4.1.3 and 4.1.4). In those circumstances it is only necessary to cite the author and the title of the work. In some instances this is done in the body of the work or it may be done in a references section of the work, but it is not the same as acknowledging when permission has been sought and given for use of a quote.

Acknowledgements for non-print materials are more varied. Written material used in a film or video programme is credited as part of the programme's end credits, where other contributions, from the provision of facilities to the format of the film stock, costume, etc., may also be credited according to the relevant contract.

In an audio production, credit may be verbal and may be made as the material is quoted or at the end of the production. It is most often placed as text in the printed wrap-around material accompanying the cassette.

Productions in other formats, such as CD-ROM or CD-I, require more thought in ensuring that the acknowledgement is either electronically tied to the material so that it tracks the material through the processes of screen display, networking and downloading, or provided as an integral part of the extract used. In some cases the provision of a separate acknowledgements section within the CD-ROM may be an acceptable alternative.

Having applied for copyright clearance, users are expected to wait for confirmation of permission before using the material. Rights holders may take some time to reply. If they do not reply within a reasonable time, say within six weeks, then a follow-up application is acceptable. Provision for a third application six weeks after that is a well-advised option before a final decision on use is taken. Should no response be generated by even that third application, the producer must weigh the risks of proceeding without confirmation against the damage that dropping the material may cause to the finished product.

Writing to the rights holder three times does not avoid infringement but it does at least provide evidence that the user has made every reasonable effort to obtain permission, in the event of a rights holder objecting after publication or release.

Users must be able to demonstrate that the effort they have made has been reasonable. Should rights holders later discover that use has been made of their material without permission, it is likely that they will seek financial return. At that point the three applications provide useful evidence of the user's good intentions – something which may greatly ease the negotiation of a reasonable fee. It is common practice in some media industries, notably broadcast television, for production budgets to carry an element designed to make provision for later payment in respect of material used without it being possible to contact the relevant rights holders before transmission.

A common myth among those seeking permission to use third party material is that they are legally covered if the letter of application carries a statement to the effect that permission will have been granted unless the rights holder replies within a specified (and often rather short) time. This is not so and in fact it often has the counter-effect of riling rights holders. It is rather like a burglar claiming an entitlement to use someone's property because no one answered his knock at the door.

4.5 COMMISSIONED MATERIAL

All commissioned work must be negotiated and written under contract specifying the nature of the work and the rights acquired. It necessitates infinitely greater contact with the author than would ordinarily be expected in using third party existing material.

The commissioning producer must be certain that the author is capable of undertaking and completing the work adequately. In some instances the author may not have a previous track record or may be moving into a particular field for the first time, particularly in the case of low-cost productions operating without the benefit of the back-up offered by established companies. Progress must be monitored carefully and scheduled to allow sufficient time for completion, handover and editing. Unrealistic deadlines impose pressure on both parties in ways that make it difficult to achieve excellence. A checklist is a useful way of ensuring that all points are covered.

Contracting a writer

1. *What is the extent of the work?*
2. *In what style is it to be written?*
3. *When must it be completed?*
4. *What rights are required? Which are essential, which are bonus?*
5. *Will it be possible to buy-out all rights in the work?*
6. *Is the author required to waive moral rights?*

Address these points before drafting the contract. The contract must specify the rights acquired by the commissioning agent. These are separate from the issue of who owns copyright. It is possible for an author to retain copyright but be unable to exploit the work personally because all other rights have been licensed to a publisher or broadcaster. It may be possible to acquire all rights in specially commissioned material, subject to financial terms being agreed. This is easier in cases involving more inexperienced authors or material of a factual nature.

Fees for commissioned material are generally higher than those charged for the right to re-use existing, third party material. The commissioning party is paying for the origination of the work and the rights of primary exploitation. The contract should not guarantee that the material will be used. It may be cut in the course of production or may not come up to the standard required.

The commissioning agent's rights in the work must be specified. The contract will break rights into layers of exploitation under option clauses which allow for payment only as and when the options are exercised. Basic rights (those essential for primary exploitation) are paid for up front as part of the commissioning contract. Secondary rights will be paid for as they are exercised.

As with all contracts, payment may be negotiated as a royalty derived from income or as a residual based upon a percentage of the original fee. Residuals are particularly favoured by broadcasters for contributors to factually based or documentary programmes. They are paid on the first sale in a given territory and can be a cost-effective way of clearing sales rights where relatively high sales can be assumed.

Writers may wish to refer to the Writers Guild to check fees and contracts before signing. No minimum rates apply to contracting written material.

4.6 LITERARY WORKS IN RECORDED FORMATS

A work does not have to be written down to be protected by copyright. An author may dictate a novel, or a politician a diary, to a personal tape-recorder and be confident that the tape-recording of the work is sufficiently permanent for the work to be protected as a literary work. No further action need be taken. In addition, the recording also enjoys protection as a sound recording and this fact must be borne in mind when reproducing material originated on tape or in a similar recorded medium. For example, in the course of making a programme about the life of a famous author, a broadcaster may discover a recording of the author telling a story – a new work as yet unpublished. The broadcaster wishes to include a long extract of the recording in the programme to be transmitted on a national network. It is agreed that the extract does not fall within the defence of fair dealing for the purposes of criticism and review and so needs to be cleared with the rights holders before use. Clearance must involve not only the literary rights in the story itself, but also the rights held in the sound recording and the performance rights held by the author.

4.7 THE COLLECTING SOCIETIES

The Copyright Licensing Agency (CLA) was set up to license photocopying of written copyright material. It is controlled by publishers and authors and it projects and protects their rights. Educational institutions, industry, government departments and libraries take licences from the CLA which allow for the photocopying of copyright material. Licensees are entitled to photocopy up to 5% of a work for the purposes of providing sufficient copies for distribution to a class of students or similar body of legitimate users. The licence allows for the photocopying of works first published in the UK, Republic of Ireland, France, Germany, Norway, Spain, Sweden, Australia, Canada, New Zealand, South Africa and the USA. It does not allow for the copying of printed sheet music, newspapers, maps, charts or books of tables, photographs divorced from text, illustrations, diagrams, bibles, liturgical works, orders of service, public examination papers, privately prepared teaching material, workbooks, industrial house journals and unpublished material. Publishers may also choose to exclude certain works from the scheme.

Photocopies generated under the terms of the CLA scheme may not be used for purposes other than those specified by the licence. One notable exclusion is for the purposes of collecting or binding together a collection of photocopied extracts from a number of articles in order to produce study packs. For that, a separate licence available under the CLA's CLARCS scheme must be obtained.

The CLA collects fees from institutions licensed by the scheme and redistributes its income proportionately among its members, through the offices of ALCS (Authors' Licensing and Collecting Society) which represents authors and PLS (Publishers Licensing Society) acting on behalf of publishers. The standard licence fee is charged annually but the CLARCS scheme levies a fee on a per project basis.

The CLA's mandate from its members currently excludes electronic and electro-copying rights of the kind required for use of materials on CD or networked formats.

Pictures

5

Because copyright protects the expression of an idea, not the idea itself, the use of information contained within a work is not restricted by copyright, though it may be protected under patent or by non-disclosure agreements. You may therefore express the ideas or describe the information in ways which convey the appropriate message yet avoid copyright infringement. Copyright is infringed if a copyright work is copied, copies issued to the public, the work is performed or shown to the public, the work is broadcast or the work is adapted. In expressing the ideas or information in a new way, producers must be careful to avoid adapting the original work in ways which infringe copyright. For example, it has already been mentioned (Chapter 4) that while a cartoon is protected by copyright, the joke it tells is not and so the same joke may be told by another cartoonist provided that the drawing (the expression of the idea) is not copied or adapted. A diagram of the workings of a water purification system is protected, but unless the system is subject to a patent then the way it works can be described or drawn anew by another person without infringing the copyright of the original author.

In many instances an author wishing to illustrate a commonplace object may find a simple drawing of the object in another book. A common argument, used particularly by authors or publishers under pressure to cut costs or to produce materials to tight deadlines, is to claim that reproducing the simple figure cannot be a breach of copyright. It is a commonplace object, they cry. 'A leaf is a leaf!' However, in choosing to reproduce another person's drawing of a leaf rather than drawing his or her own, the author will infringe copyright. The drawing of the leaf, however simple or commonplace, is protected by copyright.

This chapter looks at the use of pictures and other still visual material, including photographs, figures, diagrams and graphs. It looks at their position with regard to copyright and addresses the problem of how to locate works as well as how to clear their use. Under section 4 of the 1988

Copyright Act an 'artistic work' is defined as any 'graphic work, photograph, sculpture or collage, irrespective of artistic quality'. It is also 'a work of architecture' and 'a work of artistic craftsmanship'. A graphic work is 'any painting, drawing, diagram, map, chart or plan, and any engraving, etching, lithograph, woodcut or similar work'. The field is obviously extremely wide and, broadly, extends to include all drawings and illustrations. It also includes graphs, tables and charts. Whether producing a multimedia product or any other work, it is wise to assume that any visual image can be protected under copyright. Artistic works, like any other works, go out of copyright eventually but are protected for the life of the author plus 70 years (following EU harmonization). Before 1988 photographs were protected for 50 years from the date of first publication, so it is likely that art produced in the last 100 years is still in copyright. Clearance is needed for use of such work. It is likely that some form of clearance, either copyright clearance or access agreement, will be necessary whichever work of art you choose.

As with other material a limited amount of free use is possible. An artistic work may be used freely for the purposes of criticism and review but, as with any other use under this provision, the use must be specific in its criticism or review. Artistic works (with the exception of photographs) may also be quoted freely for the purposes of reporting current events. Photographs are not covered by this provision, an exemption which recognizes the need to protect the commercial interests of photo agencies, who depend upon the provision of photographs to newspapers and others reporting current events. An artistic work may be reproduced in a catalogue for the purposes of advertising its sale. Sculptures, buildings, models for buildings and 'works of artistic craftsmanship' permanently displayed in public may be photographed or filmed or video recorded without infringing copyright. But how should artistic works be cleared when their use is not covered by any of the above? It is useful to break them into three categories: the use of art; the use of photographs; and the use of other illustrative material, such as maps, graphs and tables.

5.1 THE USE OF ART

What is art? For rights purposes 'art' encompasses fine art, paintings, drawings, collages, sculpture, carvings, engravings, etchings and lithographs. It does not make any qualitative judgement, as work is protected regardless of quality. When using material from these categories, be aware of the rights issues raised in this section. If the work is considered to be original and falls within the definition of an artistic work, then it is protected by the law. For a work to be deemed original the only requirement is that it is not a copy.

5.1.1 FINE ART

How does a producer go about the business of using some fine art? If they are already in possession of the work, the only question to be resolved is whether or not the work is in copyright. If it is not, it may be reproduced without any worry, but if it is in copyright clearance must be sought before beginning production. An approach must be made to the rights holder or their agent and a licence negotiated. Tracking or tracing the copyright holder can sometimes be a problem, but an excellent first stop is the Design and Artists Copyright Society (DACS), a collecting and licensing society for artistic works and British artists. They are a useful starting point for finding the copyright holder for twentieth century artistic works produced by artists all over the world. If they represent the copyright holder of the work you wish to use, they will be able to issue a licence. As with any other piece of third party material, the licence granted will allow for specific use or uses. Users must ensure that the permission covers the rights they require.

When using works held in either public or private collections, producers will probably have to deal with the question of securing access as well as clearing copyright. Many works of fine art are out of copyright, but the museums and galleries holding the works, or the owners of the works, usually restrict access to them. They cannot be filmed or photographed without permission and it is usual for sometimes quite substantial fees to be charged for that permission.

Do not confuse this access permission with copyright clearance. This sort of permission covers access only. Copyright works accessed under such agreements may not be exploited without further, copyright, negotiation. Out-of-copyright works may be fully exploited with no further clearance, as long as you control all other rights in the recording. Do be careful when signing any contract allowing access to the work: it may contain conditions attempting to restrict the user's right to exploit any recording made under the access agreement. It may not be possible to refuse these conditions in negotiating access but beware of breaking the agreement. It might not be legally enforceable but it is not good practice to jeopardize relations with the collection – you might want access to the work or gallery again.

If access to the work is via a reproduction, find out whether or not the reproduction itself is a copyright work. If it is, permission will be required to reproduce it!

When looking at a work, first try to establish whether or not it is in copyright. Be clear exactly what work it is that will be used. Take a look at two examples:

A producer wishes to publish a copy of an Old Master, which is an out-of-copyright work. They have a photograph of the work, which shows the specific detail of the painting that they propose to publish, and decide that it is therefore not necessary to photograph the material again. The photograph is of sufficient quality to scan or shoot for use in the production. Yet the producer will still need to clear the use of the photograph with its rights holder, who will have rights in the exploitation of the photograph even though the painting shown in the photograph is out of copyright.

A television producer is making a film about the Tate gallery. Knowing that a film of the gallery and its exhibits already exists, it is decided to include some footage from the existing film in the new production. One extract, which has a panning shot of one of the rooms in the gallery, shows very clearly two paintings by a well-known living artist. The television producer will need to approach the producer of the first film for the right to use the existing footage (Chapter 8) and also the artists or their agents for the right to reproduce their works on screen. The original film maker is likely not to have obtained the rights in the pictures to allow for their use subsequently in other productions. They may ask that those rights should be cleared with the artist or agent direct, and insist upon that being done before granting their own sequence licence for the footage.

When clearing art works through a museum or gallery, the museum or gallery will expect producers to sign a licence which they have issued. There is nothing wrong with this as long as the licence grants the appropriate rights. Be careful to check the rights granted, as these are a constant concern when licensing copyright works. It is not uncommon for a standard licence to be issued which does not grant fully the rights requested. Sometimes the person issuing the licence may not understand what rights they are being asked to clear, especially in an interactive medium. At the point at which rights clearance is requested, be very careful to ensure that the request covers all the necessary rights and, where possible, consider acquiring options for further use. If a standard institutional licence is issued, check carefully what rights have been granted and be prepared to renegotiate the licence. As with all copyright material, permission may be refused, which is the rights holder's prerogative.

As any form of reproduction of the work is a major form of income for artists, the fees charged for the use of art can be very high. Sometimes it seems unlikely that they will ever be reduced but it is always worth trying, particularly if the source can be offered the opportunity of supplying pictures in bulk or on a regular basis. In such circumstances, reduced unit costs can often be negotiated. Broadcasters are normally expected to pay a 'flash fee' (a fee for each time the image appears on screen) and it would be rare for this charge to be waived. Producers are unlikely to persuade a gallery or museum to agree to any form of buy-out of rights but can probably negotiate options for further exploitation.

5.1.2 COMMISSIONED ARTWORK

Commissioned artwork may be required for the project, perhaps to provide a cover for a book or some graphics for a video or a CD-ROM. Who should undertake the work and can they provide the material to meet the brief and to the quality expected? Although these questions would be answered before finally commissioning an artist, it is still necessary that the contract between the artist and the production company clarifies what is to be delivered and gives details of the quality expected. It is important to give a thorough break-down of the work required in a specification attached to the contract, especially if any great quantity of work is being commissioned. If the production is being driven by tight deadlines adequate time must be written in for checking and possibly amending material after the material is handed over. If material has been prepared on computer make sure that it must be supplied in a format which allows access for amending or editing in production, particularly if the text in a map, for instance, may be changed in different language editions of the work.

Take a look at this example:

An artist provided material on a disk in a read-only format which the publisher could not manipulate. When the publisher wished to carry out standard editing the work had to be returned to the artist, who charged extra to make the changes required. The artist argued that the publisher had to accept the work as presented and was not entitled to amend the work. The publisher argued that the ability to edit the work was an essential part of producing a work of adequate quality. Eventually the publisher had to recommission the artwork with another artist, pay off the original artist and not use the original, commissioned work.

Read-only access is unworkable in a publishing operation and would be even more so in an interactive medium such as for a CD-I. It is vital that the commissioning contract should be clear about what rights the commissioning company has in the finished product. It is also essential that it does not actually commit the production company to using the work developed under contract. However careful producers are to ensure that the work done is to specification, and is acceptable in terms of quality, they may still choose not to use it. Even if the work meets the specification, changes in the course of production may make it obsolete or in some other way irrelevant. It is essential that provision for dropping the material is made clear in the contract.

5.2 THE USE OF PHOTOGRAPHS

Photographs are protected as artistic works. Under the 1988 Copyright Act the copyright holder is the photographer who takes the picture, unless there is a contract which expressly specifies an alternative. Photographs are amongst the most widely used forms of artistic works to be commissioned for use in other productions. Broadcasters and publishers use huge numbers of photographs, frequently from photo libraries and agencies, or sold by freelance photographers.

During preparations for a project a producer might decide to make use of photographs but be unsure of where to find them. There are many good and very comprehensive photographic collections which licence the use of the works they hold. Expect to pay. Contact the British Association of Picture Libraries and Agencies (BAPLA) for a list of libraries and agencies. The pictures they hold cover a variety of subjects, though a few libraries hold very specialist works. They may hold particular news or general interest items which come from newspaper, periodical and broadcasting collections. Suppliers of specialist materials tend to be smaller, many and varied and perhaps initially more difficult to locate. Photo libraries and agencies, broadcasters, museums, galleries and publishers all license the use of the photographs they hold – for a fee. If a producer has a specific industry in mind when planning a production, it is well worth approaching industrial publicity departments as they are often happy to provide material at nil or low cost.

In approaching one of these bodies for photographs there are a few points to remember. First of all, the libraries may well charge a search fee, for the time spent tracing works. Once the images have been selected, the next step is to negotiate the use and terms of use. Some collections or rights holders will only be willing to allow limited use (and if the work is in copyright, then the rights holder has that right). If the work is out of copyright, then use may at first appear to be unrestricted, but remember that access to the work will be subject to agreements which can impose restrictions on use similar to those enforced under copyright. If forced into agreeing to a limited use of a non-copyright work, consider very carefully before giving way to any temptation to break the agreement. Relationships with the holder or owner of the work may need to be maintained and, in any event, breach of contract is not something to be undertaken lightly.

Photographs are one of the most common and everyday forms of art held in private hands and can be an invaluable source of material for researchers, historians and documentary makers. People keep photographs of family and friends and of local and national occasions over the years, and when broadcasters or reporters and other writers wish to include 'real' people in their work they often value access to private photographs. Many a television programme looking back over people's lives has included a wonderful selection of family snaps that add flavour to the programme.

For anyone wishing to use photographs from private collections there are a couple of points to remember. Firstly, obtain the permission of the owner. This may not be strictly a matter of clearance, as the photographs might be out of copyright, but paying attention to securing the owner's permission may avoid the use of any other material being restricted. Check whether or not the pictures are protected by copyright and who holds the rights to them if they are. Before the 1988 Copyright Act the copyright holder in a photograph was the person who paid for the film – often, though not always, the person who commissioned the shoot. This could be a problem, for example, in the case of an author writing an article profiling the life of a famous fashion photographer who might have possession of their own fabled portfolio of fashion shots taken in the 1960s but might not control the rights. Photographs taken after the introduction of the 1988 Copyright Act, however, are the copyright of the photographer. Photographers and authors are treated alike.

5.2.1 EMPLOYING A PHOTOGRAPHER

If the photographs required for a production do not already exist or if clearance of existing material is too complicated or too expensive, a photographer may be commissioned to take photographs in response to a closely specified brief. Unless the commissioning contract assigns copyright to the commissioning producer or production company, copyright in the photgraphs will rest with the photographer. Under the 1956 Copyright Act the person or body responsible for commissioning the photograph was the copyright owner. Though that position has now changed, many commissioning bodies still cling to the view that any commission secures the copyright in the work. Many commissions are made verbally and informally and most commissioners seem content that a friendly agreement is sufficient. That is not so. Friendly agreements work perfectly well until friends fall out (and in creative industries friends seem to fall out as often as not).

Commissioning contracts need to be in writing and to be very precise in acquiring rights from the photographer. The contract must state the exact position of the rights in the photographs. It would be quite in order for the contract to assign the copyright in the photographs taken under the contract to the company requesting the work. Of course, this would have to be agreed with the photographer, and if the photographer refused to accept this, then negotiation must arrive at which rights are assigned or licensed. The commissioning producer needs, therefore, to decide precisely what rights are required in the photographs. The commissioning contract must specify precisely what photographs are to be produced, in what format they are to be handed over and when they are to be handed over.

5.2.2 SOME DO'S AND DON'TS FOR PHOTOGRAPHERS

In the absence of generally applied laws of privacy in the UK it might appear that a photographer may take pictures of whoever, whatever and wherever, but this is not strictly so. Photographs may be taken freely in a public place, even of some objects protected by copyright, but only if they are permanently displayed there. A modern sculpture placed in a street or in a shopping precinct may be photographed with impunity but the same object, displayed as part of a private collection and not in a public place, may not be photographed nor may the photograph be exploited without permission. A building may be photographed or filmed without permission, even though the architect's copyright in the plans and completed building may still be active. The photograph or film may be published, broadcast or otherwise used without permission, but the building may not be copied as a building.

Interestingly, a mural permanently displayed in a public place may not be photographed without the rights owner's consent. This exception might also apply to certain public buildings under the Official Secrets Acts of 1911, 1920 and 1989, which make it an offence to photograph many government buildings or installations such as army barracks, air force bases or naval dockyards lest the photographs prove useful to an enemy. In reality the law has been interpreted liberally in recent years and it is generally accepted that buildings which are well known to be defence establishments and with easily recognizable façades may be photographed and the results published without difficulty.

Remember that public places might not always be as public and open to access as they sometimes appear. While a landowner might not be able to prevent a photographer or film crew from shooting events from outside the property, some landowners charge access fees for film crews or photographers setting up equipment on their property. This includes some national institutions such as the National Trust and English Heritage.

5.2.3 PEOPLE IN PHOTOGRAPHS

Pictures may be taken of people in the street or in other public places, but be careful about the uses made of such photographs. It would be wise to ask anyone photographed in these circumstances to sign a release form, especially if the photographs are to be published or exploited in some way that could mean distribution to the public. If someone sees their image being used, for example in advertising, they will most certainly demand payment for its use or object to its use. Be particularly aware of the publisher's or producer's responsibility to ensure that the image is not used in circumstances that may cause embarrassment or distress.

Models (that is any sitter) employed for a photographic session should sign a release form or contract. This should not only specify the fee being paid to the model but also waive any rights the model may have in the work. If the model does not sign a waiver, the photographer or producer remains susceptible to being approached at a later date, either for more money or to restrict their use of the picture. Children (under 16 years old) cannot sign a release; their parent or guardian must sign on their behalf.

You should be aware that placing an inappropriate caption with a photograph might give sufficient cause for the subject to sue for defamation. For instance, taking a photograph of someone at the races and publishing it with the caption 'A happy punter enjoying a bet at the races' could be grounds for action. If the person at the races was a well known campaigner against gambling and their reputation suffered damage as a result, they could sue.

If a family employs a photographer to take photographs – at a wedding, for example – and the commission for the work is for the private use of the family, then the family does have the right to restrict the use of those photographs, even though the photographs are the copyright of the photographer. This provision was introduced with the 1988 Copyright, Designs and Patents Act. In the mid 1980s photographs taken of the Royal Family for use on the royal Christmas cards were acquired by newspapers and published. It was considered seriously by Parliament and consequently the quasi-moral right of privacy in privately commissioned photographs was introduced. In recent times newspapers have been heavily criticized for the publication of photographs of prominent people taken without consent and knowledge. At present there is nothing to prevent this, as there is no general law of privacy in the UK, though some other member states of the EU (notably France) do protect the privacy of the citizen. The UK right to privacy only concerns **commissioned** photographs and the person who commissioned them. However, the Press Complaints Commission has its own code on this subject, and politicians are always happy to express concern about such photographs, so changes may yet come. Medical photographs are an important category to fall under the general concepts of privacy. Care should be taken to secure the patient's consent and wherever possible the photograph should be taken so as not to disclose the patient's identity. Disclosure, apart from being an intrusion into private life that none of us would much care for, could be a breach of confidence.

Most people are somewhat intuitively aware of the laws on obscenity. It is an offence under the Obscene Publications Acts (1959 and 1964) to publish any obscene materials. Publication means distribution, lending, circulating, selling, giving, hiring, or offering for sale or hire. The courts must judge if material is obscene – a difficult judgement. Over the years society has accepted the publication of increasingly explicit material, and many photographs published today would probably have been judged 'obscene' 60 years ago. While it is often a matter of common sense to decide if subject matter may be judged obscene or not, producers must be aware of this as an issue.

5.3 OTHER ILLUSTRATIVE MATERIAL

Producers might be interested in using illustrative material which would not normally be classified as 'artistic': architectural drawings and designs, diagrams, maps, tables, graphs or charts, or any other illustrative work. They can all be protected by copyright and users will need to clear permission to use or prepare the work for publication or production.

5.3.1 DESIGNS

The question of designs is complex. A design drawing is protected as an artistic work and should not be copied as a drawing without permission. To reproduce a design drawing or diagram, seek permission from the copyright holder. If permission is granted check that it covers adequately the use requested. The owners of design rights may have more reason that many other rights holders to refuse permission for their work to be reproduced. They may feel that use increases the opportunities for rival businesses to compete more aggressively.

5.3.2 MAPS

Maps may be protected works under copyright. For some producers this might seem bizarre; for many, a map hardly seems an artistic work at all. However, if the work is at all original in its execution it can be protected by copyright. To reproduce any map, seek permission from the rights holder. It can seem a difficult thing to create a new map – after all, towns and physical geographical features must be placed accurately or the map is defective – but in so far as any new drawing of a map is not a copy of another, it may well be considered a new work and afforded copyright protection.

The Ordnance Survey (OS) is the best known of copyright holders in maps of the British Isles. It sets specific rate cards for the use of works and these are normally non-negotiable. Costs vary according to the size of the map as reproduced, its scale and the proportion of the extract to the original map as a whole, as well as to the more usual parameters of print run and exploitation rights. The OS claims an underlying copyright in all maps produced of the UK, so that, for instance, town route guides are based upon OS maps and the OS licenses their use. In using any of the many town guides, producers will have to clear rights both with the publishers of the town guide and with the OS.

There are other people and organizations who are rights holders in maps, all of whom control rights in their work. The fee paid for any use is negotiable and the rights granted are negotiable. Ensure that the rights granted allow sufficient use of the material and that this is specified in writing.

5.3.3 TABLES, GRAPHS AND CHARTS

Tables, graphs or charts which are found in the body of a text are treated as separate copyright works, distinct from any copyright existing in the book, journal or article as a whole. A producer who wishes to reproduce one of these works will need to seek permission to do so just as with any other, seemingly more substantial piece of third party material. The process is exactly the same as seeking permission to reproduce any other copyright work. Rights holders normally make a charge for the reproduction of these works. Again, be certain that the rights granted are sufficient.

Producers may choose to use the information contained within graphical, tabular or representational works and express it in a new way. This does not infringe the rights of the rights holder. Copyright does not protect ideas: it protects the expression of ideas. In many instances it is extremely difficult to separate information from its expression, but in a graph or table the information is often obvious and quite distinct from its graphical representation. In many instances it is comparatively simple to extract the data and rewrite it, avoiding infringement.

5.4 ACKNOWLEDGEMENTS

When reproducing any artwork or photograph or illustrative material, producers must acknowledge the copyright holder. The form for these acknowledgements normally follows the form of any other copyright acknowledgement needed for other work: credit the author or creator, the title of the work, the original publisher (where applicable) and the year of origination. Frequently photographic credits are extremely short and only acknowledge the photographer and agency by whom the photograph was supplied.

Illustrative material

Copyright and access rights in photographic or artistic materials may co-exist on several levels, all of which must be cleared before the illustration may be used. Here is a useful checklist to follow in clearing illustrative materials.

1. *The photograph:*
   Has use been cleared with the copyright owner?
   Has use been cleared with the owner of the print being used?
2. *The subject:*
   Has the subject been engaged on a model release form or other form of written rights release?
   Has the owner of rights in a physical object (painting, sculpture, etc.) granted release?

Has the owner of the object (e.g. the collector rather than the artist) granted permission?

3. *Location access:*
   Has access to the object been approved?
   Under what terms?
4. *Privately commissioned photographs:*
   Has the individual who commissioned the photographs granted permission?

Music

6

In the opinion of the late Duke Ellington there are only ever two types of music: good and bad. Producers of multimedia works know that there are four: commercial recordings, library (or mood or production) music, commissioned works and live performances.

Music can be one of the most attractive and, simultaneously, one of the most troublesome of the media options you can select to enhance your production. Each of the four categories listed carries its own distinct advantages and drawbacks and needs to be approached on its own terms. The complex rights position that applies to musical works generally arises from the fact that the medium itself is part of a highly developed and sophisticated industry that exists solely to extract revenue returns from the commercial exploitation of intellectual property rights though systems of blanket, collective and individual licensing.

6.1 COMMERCIAL RECORDINGS

The use of commercial recordings seems to be an easy way of enhancing the production values of any multimedia work but they have to be used with care and must be cleared early in the production schedule if they are not to become a liability.

Commercial recordings of music are themselves the product of a complex web of interacting rights, and so using a commercial recording of a chart song or a classical piece will involve you in negotiating clearances at a number of levels in the original recording. In a chain with so many possible links, the possibility of the total clearance breaking down is strong. Whatever happens, clearance will be time consuming and probably expensive.

To illustrate the problem: assume that you want to use a popular recording of a song in your production. At the most basic level the recording will have three layers of copyright: the music, the lyrics and the recording itself. In addition the performer and possibly the backing singers or band will control rights in their performance or will have granted control of the performing rights to the record company (which cuts out one step in your clearance of the material).

The composer of the music will own copyright in their musical work and you will have to obtain their permission in order to use the recording. It is usual for composers to transfer control of rights in the music by either assignment or exclusive licence to their publisher, and so another link in the chain is established. Approaching the publisher may be more difficult than it sounds for many publishers control rights in one territory only (say the UK) and you may wish to sell or distribute your product in any number of territories, where publishing rights may be controlled or leased to another publisher or a sub-publisher member of a multinational group.

In practice, it is usual for publishers to mandate the Mechanical-Copyright Protection Society (MCPS) to license the exercise of the mechanical rights in the UK (the right to make recordings of the composition). You may find that some publishers prefer to remain outside the MCPS and you will have to approach these direct.

A song's lyrics are regarded as a separate copyright work separate from the music. Even if a singer–songwriter has written both music and lyrics, they might well be controlled separately by two different publishers. Separate clearance will, therefore, be required for the lyrics. If you are using a commercial recording, check the publishing credits on the sleeve or liner notes for details of who controls rights in the composition and lyrics.

So far you will have cleared rights in two of the three main elements of a commercial recording but the record company will itself control rights in the recording of the song as a recording. These, too, will have to be cleared before you are able to include the recording in your production. But be careful: the record company and the publisher have so far only granted the right to play the song in this recorded version.

For use in a video, film or multimedia production where the music will be played in partnership with a visual image, moving or still, you will also need to clear the synchronization right – the right to dub the recording to play simultaneously with the image. This right is controlled by the recording company, in the case of the recording, and by the publisher, in the case of the composition, by whom (as a general rule) it is commonly delegated to the MCPS or its equivalent in another territory.

Such a complicated chain of rights clearances has clear implications for the selection and use of commercial recordings which go beyond the hard work and effort involved in tracking, contacting and negotiating with a variety of rights holders. At each link in the chain you will encounter rights holders properly anxious to secure a commercial return on their property and, crucially, rights holders who are not themselves fully in control of the works they own. The control exercised by recording companies, for example, is limited to the extent of the rights granted under contracts with their own artists. In an industry where image is often everything, in which riders to concert contracts may even insist upon specific brands of peanuts for the after-gig party, many artists insist upon tight restrictions upon the use of their material – and not always for reasons you might consider valid. It is not unknown for bands dedicated to a rock-and-roll lifestyle of considerable ferocity suddenly to insist upon viewing educational programmes on particle physics before deciding to grant or withhold approval for the dubbing of their recordings. Use of recordings in particular contexts might be ruled out because of restrictions imposed by the artists, often for the sake of their promotional image. Others, including classical conductors, might insist that their work, or work conducted by them, may only be dubbed in programmes in which they feature as the subject of a review or biography.

The recording companies themselves might also add to your confusion. Many choose to be represented by MCPS for synchronization rights but many (particularly the bigger companies) do not. This means having to contact the company direct and in many cases leads to a clearance trail that tracks through a UK subsidiary of a US major label. However helpful the UK operations wishes to be, they could find themselves tied to company policy developed in the US or able to grant only UK rights or not able to act independently for certain artists.

If after all this you do succeed in getting clearance, confirm it straight away. Circumstances may alter, either through changing company policy or through changing artists' contracts, so that tracks available comparatively easily today might become impossible to clear if you leave confirmation to the day after you have completed editing.

Commercial recordings, therefore, can be difficult to clear along a complicated rights network. They can be expensive. They might also be impossible to clear because of rights restrictions imposed by the artists. They must be approached with care. Yet they remain attractive because of the sense of production values that they can bring and because they offer the possibility of a witty, ironic, sentimental counterpoint to the visual image.

6.2 LIBRARY (OR PRODUCTION) MUSIC

Library music is also commonly known as mood music and is the simplest form of recorded music to include in any production. It is created for one purpose only: to be used in audio-visual productions. A growing number of recording companies specialize in providing library music, making it available via series of CDs which are mailed to production houses and producers and to anyone else who might be interested in using the product. No charge is payable until the work is used in production.

Library music at one time enjoyed an unenviable reputation of being boring wallpaper music of the kind used in lifts. It was restricted in scope and the catalogues held little of either classical or out-of-copyright material. That is now changing fast and a broad range of classical and out-of-copyright works is becoming more widely available. So, unless you require a particular interpretation of a Beethoven quartet, you might be better advised to find one in a library catalogue than to use a commercially released recording.

Library music is simple to use. Its one similarity with wallpaper these days is the fact that it is bought off the roll, in lengths of 29 or 59 seconds. You then inform the library company of your use – sometimes direct, sometimes via MCPS – and pay according to a set rate. Clearance is guaranteed in advance and nothing could be simpler. Or could it?

Well, yes, some care does still need to be taken. It is easy to assume that the logistical ease of obtaining clearance will necessarily be reflected in a commercial ease of paying for it but that is not the case. As library music is generally sold in 29-second sections, 29 seconds will accrue one unit's charge while 31 seconds will accrue a charge of two units. Be sensitive to this and stay on the right side of the unit cost wherever possible, though in synchronizing music with footage you sometimes have to cross the divide between one charge unit and another. The units are not cumulative. It is common practice in educational productions, for instance, to use a music sting to cue students when moving to another section of accompanying text. Using a dozen such 2- or 3-second stings in your production would not accumulate 24 or 36 seconds of paid time. Each sting would be licensed separately, for a total fee of 12 times the unit rate.

This presents an intriguing scenario for multimedia productions in which a single piece of music may be physically recorded once only, but might be designed to play any number of times under hypertext direction. Should that be licensed as a single use or, as the repeat plays are under direct control of the production's own internal logic links, should the licence cover the number of times the software directs that the piece should be played? At present the position is under review. For production music, only the duration of the dubbed extract is taken into account, not the number of times it plays under the direction of the production's software. For commercial recordings, however, the position is more fluid with each case being assessed individually until an industry-approved approach is formed.

Networked systems are also treated differently from CD-ROM and CD-I formats. Networked use will be assessed on a per case basis, taking into account variables such as the number of sites having access to the system, how often access is likely to be used, how often the system is likely to be updated and how much music is going to be used.

Current rates may be obtained from MCPS and are presented in the form of a rate card which takes account of the nature of your production, its presentation, distribution and audience. Copies are readily available.

6.3 COMMISSIONED MUSIC

Commissioning music might seem to be an expensive and complicated way of getting a soundtrack or theme tune for your production. For most of us it is the kind of thing more usually associated with big budget productions. The reality is that, in many cases, commissioned music can be a relatively inexpensive and trouble-free way of creating a soundtrack. Chapter 7 gives details of contracting musicians, a field which overlaps to some extent with the business of commissioning music. Read section 7.2 in conjunction with this one.

The first thing to consider is the category of music you wish to commission. Obviously, for many productions a single composer/performer may be enough without the need to commission a large-scale piece recorded by a full orchestra, though in some cases even that may be less troublesome and give you greater options for sales exploitation than using commercial recordings. In one instance involving a prime-time television police drama series in which the central character was a lover of 1930s jazz, the producer found it better to commission and doctor (with dubbed clicks and scratches) a modern pastiche rather than use the original gramophone recordings.

Your options will range from the many local composer/arranger/performers who are easily available in most areas, to well-known and regarded composers with many credits to their name. The choice is down to you and your budget. What cannot be avoided is the need to think carefully before briefing composers on what you want them to produce.

First you must engage the composer and agree the commission, including the use to which the work will be put. This will require you, as always with rights acquisition, to think through the use to which you hope to put your own production. At what audience is it aimed? How will it reach that audience? In which territories? The rights you can acquire will depend on the composer you are commissioning. Music commissioned for a relatively low-cost production would probably be contracted on an all-rights basis which allows you to use the music however you wish and will not impose restrictions on the subsequent exploitation of the production. Composers represented by publishers and/or agents will probably not be available for work on all-rights contracts and your commissioning contract will, as part of the negotiating process, reflect that. The negotiation will represent the resolution of the tension existing between the rights you wish to acquire and your production budget. At the barest minimum you must make sure that you are free to synchronize the music with your production and to exploit it without restraint in the territories and media you require.

6.4 LIVE PERFORMANCES

Live performances fall into three main contract categories for performers and two main categories for rights clearance.

6.4.1 PERFORMER CATEGORIES

For performers, the Musicians Union agrees rates for musicians (playing solo or in groups or orchestras) and for singers (either solo or choral) where they are not required to play a character in performance. The virtuosi in a small chamber group or quartet are likely to be represented by the Incorporated Society of Musicians. Singers playing a role in opera, or in other dramatico-musical works in which they perform as characters in the drama, are represented by Equity, which also represents the dancers you use in recording a ballet or dance musical.

6.4.2 RIGHTS CLEARANCE CATEGORIES

For clearing rights in the music itself, productions are categorized as being either concert or dramatico-musical. For concert performances you should clear rights through MCPS. Dramatico-musical productions (operas, musicals and ballets) can only be cleared by dealing direct with the music publisher.

In clearing live performances, the Performing Right Society and the Music Publishers Association are both good first ports of call. They can provide useful information on whether or not the music is still in copyright (which can be more difficult than it seems – remember that an arrangement of a traditional or out-of-copyright piece can be in copyright even if the original is not), who controls the rights and whether it falls into the dramatico-musical category.

For any performance, whether the work is out of copyright or not, it is likely that you will have to pay the publisher an additional premium or hire fees for the right to record a performance using the published score. Copyright works will carry the additional cost of clearing synchronization rights (which will vary according to the nature of your production and its exploitation) and mechanical duplication rights covering videogram duplication and release.

6.5 THE CLEARANCE PROCESS

The music business is a highly developed and sophisticated industry which depends for its profits on exploiting rights in works which are produced by and exploited through rapidly changing technologies. The industry itself reflects its technology. It is awake to new opportunities for rights exploitation provided by the introduction of the newer electronic media and responds quickly to approaches for clearance.

Some other trades, perhaps most notably some parts of the book trade, respond more slowly to requests for copyright clearance, insist upon written communication and refuse to negotiate on the phone. For them the fax is an irritant. Nothing could be further from the attitudes you are likely to encounter in clearing music. Almost without exception, clearances will be agreed and negotiated by phone. Delays will be kept to a minimum and the fax is the preferred means of communication. All of this is wonderful but it also imposes a discipline on the producer seeking clearance. You must be prepared to talk clearly about the rights you need and be confident in negotiating a price. Familiarity with technology has resulted in fast, positive communication when clearing music rights and it is also reflected in the industry's sharp-minded approach to licensing. Licences for run-of-the-mill clearances are extremely specific about the number of copies that can be made, the country of manufacture, type of sale and broadcast, cassette or electronic delivery. Some newer licences also specify analogue or digital rights, reflecting the industry's awareness of the copying possibilities offered by digital systems. You must think through exactly what rights you need to license before approaching the rights holder.

The rights holder, or the collecting society to which control has been delegated, will want to know details of the music you have selected for production and the way in which you intend to use it. To supply this information you will need to keep a full and proper record of the selection and use of recordings, held as part of the production paperwork. This record is known as the music cue sheet (Figure 6.1) and is a written account of each track. It gives details of the artist, composer, recording label and serial number, track listing and duration of the extract used. It also specifies whether the recording was used as background or featured music in the production. Featured recordings can be heard by participants in the production. Music playing on a radio during a domestic scene in a drama can be heard by the actors playing the scene and is classified as featured, even though the radio may be playing quietly in the background. Background use covers recordings dubbed to accompany visual images in which the participants cannot hear the music – behind narrative tracks, for instance. Recordings chosen as theme music must be listed as a separate category.

Most rights holders will request details of the track as shown in the cue sheet, the scene it accompanies, the total duration of your production and the rights you wish to clear. They may also ask to know the length and proportion of the total music content to the production as a whole. MCPS will then feed that information into a standard mathematical formula to produce a licence fee. Recording companies and publishers will use it to construct a negotiating position.

Music Cue Sheet

Production title:			Release date:		Page No:	of

Production Company Details: (Name, Address, Contact name and telephone number.)

Music Title	Composer/Arranger	Publisher	Performers	Label and No.	Category	Use	Duration
That's the way to do it	Mr Punch	Crocodile Publishing	Punch and Judy	Cry Baby Records WAA	P	F	27"

Category codes: B = Background   F = Featured
                  S = Signature   C = Commercial

Use Codes: P = Production music
                CR = Commercial recording
                V = Video/Film soundtrack

Use codes to specify how the music is used: (Use column)

e.g.   B = Background
      F = Featured
      S = Signature
      C = Commissioned

and type of recording: (Category column)

e.g.   P = Production/Mood/Library music
      CR = Commercial recording
      V =

Points to remember:

Each use of a work must be timed separately, include in film extracts timings for music.
Featured music is music audible to those appearing in the production.
Background music is audible only to viewers of the programme.
Synchronization rights apply also to commissioned material.

Figure 6.1   Music cue sheet

In practice, you will find that many recording companies have authorised MCPS to act on their behalf in licensing mechanical rights. In that case, MCPS will be your one-stop shop for the clearance you require and might be able to license your complete production. Several major recording and publishing companies, however, reserve control of mechanical rights, which means that you will have to contact and deal with each direct. This can mean that, although the mechanical rights are available, the publishing rights are not (and vice versa) so do not finally clear a track until you are certain of clearing all its elements. One historical production linked images from the current events of a year to a soundtrack of popular hits from the same year. The format gave rise to a particularly complicated 'catch-22' when it became apparent that the recordings of one well known group were restricted but the publisher's rights were not. A possible way around the problem, while still retaining the link between the song and the image, would have been to license a sound-alike recording from a music library. However, the route was blocked when it was discovered that the publisher did not license the work for performance by sound-alikes. The sound track had to be re-cut.

Having read so far you may well be wondering how it is that any television production involving music ever gets under way at all. The answer lies in the arrangements that the UK radio and television broadcasters have with the music industry via a number of blanket or collective licensing agreements. These general licences allow the broadcasters to transmit, within the UK and allowing for some limited arrangements for fringing reception in certain adjacent parts of mainland Europe, any music represented by the collective licensing organizations. In return for an annually negotiated fee the broadcasters are free to broadcast any of the music included in their schedules, subject to full returns logging transmission details. The annual blanket licence fees are then split proportionately between members of the collecting societies. If your production is being made to be screened by a broadcaster you should ask which blanket agreements they have in place and what rights they cover. Their agreements are likely to cover most or all of your use of music and allow you to concentrate upon clearing only those elements that are not covered.

The collective agreements in place between broadcasters and the societies cover only the UK, however, and you must be aware of this when clearing musical content. It is increasingly the case that broadcasters insist upon programmes being cleared for exploitation in the world market. Additional or extended clearances will be needed for those territories not covered by the UK agreements. It is at this point that the clearance most often breaks down. Freed from the control offered under the blanket system, recording companies or their artists may chose to restrict use of their work outside the UK. This can affect both productions which feature music as central to their audience appeal and those (such as general documentary, educational or nature programming) which include music as background accompaniment or as part of a location recording. Several prominent British television series which relied upon music for a good deal of their artistic integrity and appeal, such as *The Singing Detective* (which used nostalgic recordings of popular songs) and *Tutti Frutti* (in which the central characters were in a rock-and-roll group), have had to be re-edited for sale or broadcast outside the UK.

In another case, a documentary programme which followed a traveller across the United States ran into problems because of the inclusion of music playing on a juke-box during a scene set in the foyer of a brothel. Even though the music being played was not central to the scene nor to the documentary as a whole, sale or broadcast of the programme outside the UK was prevented because the artist's representatives refused to license the showing of his recording in such a location. The fact that the music was playing during the scene and recorded as part of it meant that it could not be edited out or re-dubbed without cutting the visuals. Faced with a choice between releasing an edited version of the documentary and restricting its use to UK transmission only, the broadcasters in this case came down in favour of restricted use.

The case is interesting because it illustrates the problems that programme makers face in making location recordings when not all elements of production can be under their complete control. Chapter 1 discussed why it is difficult to use a defence of an 'insubstantial part' in using musical works. The concept that each note has to fight hard for its place in the composition means that quoting even small phrases can be an infringement if the phrase carries the recognizable melody of the complete work. Popular television game shows like *Name That Tune*, in which contestants compete to name popular tunes from hearing only a few notes, evidence how much information can be gleaned from only a very small element of any tune.

This makes life difficult for programme makers on location recording. In the studio, music can be cleared before use and recorded on a separate track so that, should a problem arise unexpectedly, it can be edited out without also losing the commentary or the accompanying visual image. Life is much more difficult for live studio work or for location recordings. Recognizing this, the 1988 Copyright Act makes provision for the incidental inclusion of musical works in other artistic works, sound recordings, films, broadcasts or cable programmes. (Videos, CDs, networked systems and multimedia productions fall under these categories.) The incidental inclusion of musical works is not an infringement of copyright.

For the defence of incidental inclusion to hold good, the Act says that musical works or lyrics are not to be regarded as being incidentally included if they are deliberately included. For practical purposes, this tautology should be regarded as pointing to two areas:

1. Any collusion between the programme maker and the person or persons performing the music or playing the recording.
2. The possibility of re-editing in post-production.

6.5.1 COLLUSION

Of the two, the first is the more important. It means that a programme maker cannot decide with a busker, for instance, or a school choir, or a DJ or someone putting another coin in a juke box, what musical selection they are about to make. It also means that if the recording can be stopped and restarted using a different musical selection, then the defence of incidental inclusion may be weakened. Where it holds good is in cases in which the visual image or spoken soundtrack cannot be repeated. For instance, coverage of a football match at which the public address system plays a record would be held to have included the musical work incidentally. A band striking up at the approach of a dignitary would similarly be outside the programme maker's control. The broadcaster cannot stop the action for the goal to be scored again or for dignitaries to retrace their steps back to the aircraft.

6.5.2 POST-PRODUCTION EDITING

Post-production opportunities may weaken the defence of incidental inclusion in cases where re-editing is possible. Each case needs to be judged on its merit. In the case of the record playing on the juke box, one would be weighing up the possibilities that existed at the time of recording on location and the possibility of removing the music from the final programme. There is a school of thought that says that any recorded programme offers the programme maker the choice of including the music or not and, therefore, no recorded programme can, strictly speaking, claim that inclusion was truly incidental. Perhaps this view is extreme but it is, nevertheless, a useful indication of how limited the defence could be in certain circumstances.

6.6 COLLECTIVE LICENSING SOCIETIES

For music, the representation of rights holders is broken down between those bodies that license recording (mechanical) rights and those that license public performance rights (including broadcasting). Some represent the composers and publishers, others the recording industry.

The Music Publishers Association (MPA) represents the major UK music publishers and wholly owns the Mechanical-Copyright Protection Society (MCPS).

MCPS is a collection agency which licenses the rights of its members. Most are publishers but membership is not confined to them. MCPS also represents the rights of composers, other copyright owners and recording companies. Though some of the major labels have chosen not to be represented via MCPS, the organization does represent a very wide range of rights interests and is an extremely valuable point of contact when clearing music. It is the nearest we can get to one-stop clearance for music.

MCPS licenses the mechanical reproduction rights owned by its members. The public performance rights in a musical composition are licensed by the Performing Right Society (PRS), who license and distribute fees for the public performance of music. Composers and publishers assign their rights in a musical work to PRS. Public performance rights range from local concerts to broadcasts on the national networks.

The recording industry is represented through two similar bodies. The British Phonographic Industry (BPI) performs a similar role to the MPA on behalf of recording companies. The recording industry equivalent to the PRS is Phonographic Performance Ltd (PPL) which licenses public performance rights in commercial recordings.

Video Performance Ltd (VPL) licenses the use of music videos for screening as public performances or broadcasts in the UK.

People

7

If you use any audio-visual material in your multimedia project you may well wish to have contributions from 'real' people in your programmes. The ways in which you use people and what they are doing in the recording affect the ways in which they are normally contracted and what they are paid for their contribution. This chapter divides them into four categories – actors, musicians, professional broadcasters and members of the public – and gives a breakdown of the rights they hold and how to contract them. It also gives advice on the use of 'employees' in a production.

7.1 ACTORS, SINGERS AND DANCERS

If you decide to record a dramatization, you would be best advised to use professional actors to perform in it. Although it is no longer legal to operate a closed shop many actors will not work with non-professionals; also you would probably prefer your programme to look professional and the way to achieve that is to employ professionals. Actors work within the agreed rules that Equity (British Actors Equity Association, the actors' trade union) negotiates with the various producers of audio visual materials. Independent television and video producers can contract actors under the PACT agreement (Producers Alliance for Cinema and Television). The broadcasters contract actors under their own agreements; separate ones exist for the BBC and ITV.

There is justification for not using professional actors in certain circumstances. You might be making a programme about social workers or for social work training and you wish to see real people 'role-playing' in order to learn better how to deal with specific issues. In this instance you obviously want to use as many real people as possible. This situation shows that there is not always a clear boundary between what members of the public do and what actors do.

In order to decide whether or not you should engage professional actors to carry out role-plays, you need to think carefully about what it is you are trying to get out of the programme. Is it that you want to examine the 'real people' and the way that they learn or react to situations, or are you simply illustrating an issue? If it is a case of purely illustrating a subject you should engage the professionals.

The first question to consider when engaging actors is what precisely do you want them to do? Do you have a script to work to? Do you wish to audition the actors? How long do you expect them to work for? In the case of a dance, do you intend to employ a professional choreographer? A professional actor will want answers to these questions before taking on the work. Most would expect to be paid a fee for attending an audition and to receive expenses for any extended travel.

Next you have to consider the use you propose to make of the contribution. You should decide which rights are required from the final programme before engaging the actor and negotiate for the acquisition of those rights before work begins.

Possible uses

Here is a checklist of possible uses:

1. *Do you propose to broadcast the work?*
2 *How do you propose to broadcast the work?*
   by normal tv or radio?
   by cable?
   by satellite?
3. *Are you producing a video?*
4. *Are you producing an interactive product?*
5. *Do you wish to sell the finished programme:*
   on video through shops?
   to broadcasters overseas?
   for use in educational institutions?
6. *Is the programme to be shown in the cinema?*

The performers, whether they are professional or not, have rights in their performance and you need to contract them appropriately to allow for the exploitation required of the programme. As with any other third party material the rights in a performance by an actor are controlled by the actor. As the producer, you should issue a contract to the actor that gives you the right to exploit the programme in the way you wish, including the right not to use the work if you so wish. The rights in the performance can be granted in as limited a form as any other piece of third party material; thus the actor can limit the rights by territory, by time, by numbers of copies allowed to be issued, by media (issue on videocassette, issue by some form of interactive media, sale for educational exhibition only, sale through retail outlets, transmission by satellite or by terrestrial transmitter, etc.) and so on. The rights acquired will affect the fee payable.

Equity negotiates on behalf of the profession to agree minimum rates of pay for the work done by actors and for the level of fee payable for each form of exploitation of their work. The rates payable for performances vary considerably depending on which agreement the producer is bound to apply; they range from a minimum fee of c. £200 per week for work in a provincial theatre to a minimum fee of c. £400 for a week's work with the BBC, which allows for one domestic transmission only. These figures are minimum payments and producers should expect actors with commercial muscle to negotiate at levels above this.

What is payable for further use of the performance? Broadcasters have always had to pay repeat fees to actors. This came about due to the fact that in the early days of broadcasting it was not possible to keep recordings of the programmes. Therefore when the BBC, for example, wished to repeat a play on a Wednesday that was first transmitted on a Sunday, on the next Wednesday the actors had to be brought into the studios to perform again. They were consequently paid a second fee; thus when the technology was developed for recording the performances, the actors felt that if they were not paid a repeat fee they would be losing out on earnings. This set the precedent for paying actors for the further use of their work. The repeat fees or residuals, as they are often called, are calculated as a percentage of the original fee paid. The percentage payable for repeat transmissions within the term of the contract is usually 50–80%.

After the contract period has expired, and depending on which Equity agreement it was issued under, the repeat fees either rise dramatically or the right to repeat must be cleared with the artist. This gives artists the facility to stop a showing of a work which they might wish to forget. If you feel the life of your recording is likely to be longer than about 2 years, try to buy a longer life up front.

7.2 MUSICIANS

If you wish to engage musicians to work for you, you will need to issue them with a contract. There are points in common with this contract and any other contract for a person. Never commit yourself to using the work performed by the person. As with actors, you would be advised to use professional musicians if you wish to record musical performances. Again there are times when you would wish to record with amateurs but you should always pay reasonable fees. In order to engage a group of musicians, first choose your artists. You might find that the services of a 'fixer' will help in this instance. Fixers choose and assemble a group of musicians for you. They pay the musicians on your behalf and will therefore be contracted to provide the services of the musicians. They will not receive individual contracts from you. You can find music fixers by contacting music agencies or the Musicians Union (MU). The MU recognizes certain individuals as fixers or 'contractors' who have signed an agreement to ensure that any recording contracts offered to individual musicians comply with the union agreement pertaining to that specific engagement and agreeing to pay the musicians promptly within 28 days of the engagement. Fixers are obviously paid a fee for the fixing service and, as they are often also performers themselves, they are paid a performance fee too. Normally the musical director (MD), leader or conductor is paid a higher basic fee than the musicians

Musicians work to agreements agreed by the unions (either the Musicians Union or the Incorporated Society of Musicians, a professional association) and they should be paid union rates. These are often non-negotiable and allow for fixed hours of work. You should therefore be well prepared to work with them so that time is not wasted. Have a clear idea of what you wish to record in the session and agree this with your conductor, fixer, MD or leader. The fixer or MD can advise you whether all you have planned is achievable in the time allowed. If it is not and you go into overtime, you will be left with a substantial bill. You may also be forced into working two sessions with your musicians. Also, when you engage musicians to work for you, do not forget to clear the music that they play for the use you envisage (Chapter 6).

Musicians are usually paid porterage for the transportation of large or bulky instruments. They are also paid doubling fees for playing more than one instrument during the session. Doubling is the practice of employing, for example, one percussionist to play both drums and glockenspiel during the recording session, neither instrument being heard at the same time as the other. This is not the same as employing one musician to lay down several tracks, each on a different instrument, which are then heard as a single piece of music – a practice known colloquially as multi-tracking. The MU frowns on the practice of multi-tracking and employing fewer musicians than are needed to play all the instruments heard at any one time on the track. You might also have to pay for instrument hire and to hire sheet music from the music publisher.

Recording music is a specialized exercise and you would be well advised to ensure that you have the right facilities before you start. Do you have access to a music recording studio or do you propose to hire one? When recording with a group of musicians you need an adequate supply of microphones and should ensure that the studio has enough channels to balance the sound properly. If you are not technically gifted yourself, do employ technicians who understand sound balancing. Any problems arising from technical problems will probably lead to needing your musicians to work overtime.

Many people these days wish to engage a single musician/composer who works with a synthesizer and who composes and performs on that instrument. It can be an advantageous way of working if the music fits the bill. You will have to issue the artist with a contract which commissions the composition of the music and which covers the rights you require in the performance. You can limit the rights you take in the composition to those required for the project but it would be normal to ask for a total assignment of copyright. It must be said here that many composers dislike this practice (Chapter 6). When it comes to contracting the performance you do not have to engage the artist under union terms and conditions if the musician is playing a synthesizer, because the MU does not recognize synthesizers and so you can mutually agree a fee and what that fee covers. Thus the restraints imposed by the union agreements will not necessarily affect you. You will not necessarily save money with this method, as the agreed fee will normally be within union rates, but the hours of work and the rights you can acquire will be more flexible than those agreed by the unions.

There are disadvantages to employing a synthesizer player. You will have problems if you wish to engage both ordinary musicians and a synthesizer player but the synthesizer impersonates another musical instrument. MU members are banned from working with synthesizer players in this instance and if you did manage to get a musician to work for you in this way they could be blacked by other musicians. If a synthesizer player decides to record some traditional music performed by a traditional musician and then manipulate that piece of music to provide the sound required, the musician would have to be paid a session fee and you would have to abide by union agreements when using that contribution.

If you wish to engage a musical group or band, the rates payable vary depending on whether the group considers itself to be represented by the MU or by Equity. Equity would normally represent a singing group and the MU would represent musicians. The distinctions between them can become blurred but, as a rule of thumb, a musical group should be contracted in line with MU agreements.

If you decide to record with a pop group which has signed a recording agreement with a record company, you will need to check whether or not that contract allows you to make your recording. Some record companies will control all the recordings made by the artists, even those that are unlikely to form any sort of competition with the work done for the record company. If the record company perceives the work done in your recording to be promotional, then they are likely to allow you to record whatever you like; however, they are unlikely to allow you to sell your recording. Record companies may also offer to pay the performance fees of artists when producing a promotional production, but this will not save you from the necessity of clearing further use, which they may restrict and if they do not you will have to pay union rates for the further use.

In recent years some broadcasters and recording companies have become increasingly frustrated with the Musicians Union and its disinclination to change practices in order to come into line with what some see as a more modern way of working. They have decided to go abroad to make recordings and to use local musicians. These recording sessions often involve no union conditions at all and the broadcasters and recording companies can use the recordings with little restriction. It appears that these recordings are as good quality as ones made in the UK, but the savings made on rights fees have to be balanced against the cost of going abroad. It would probably prove prohibitive except for quite large-scale productions.

7.3 PROFESSIONAL BROADCASTERS

Professional broadcasters will help to give your programme a polished finish, be they presenters or commentary narrators, but they do not do the job for free and you will need to negotiate reasonable fees with the chosen artist. Some negotiate for themselves but most of them are represented by agents. You do not need to work to union agreements when booking a presenter or narrator, although Equity does represent many of these artists. ITV has long issued these artists with Equity contracts but the BBC does not. Try not to engage these artists under Equity rules. When producing a recording for an independent production you are free to negotiate the fee without recourse to union agreements.

As you will probably be engaging these artists under terms and conditions mutually decided you will have to give careful consideration to the terms and conditions of the engagement. You could try to offer an all-rights contract to presenters or narrators but there are some likely drawbacks with this. Professional broadcasters will expect to be paid a considerably enhanced fee in return for granting all-rights. This fee may be prohibitive for you, so you will have to reconsider the rights you require. Some agents and artists will refuse to sign an all-rights contract, so you will be pushed into issuing a different contract that gives only limited rights in the contribution. Draw up a contract which allows you to exploit the material you record in the way you need.

If you do have to issue a contract taking only limited rights in the contribution, you must obviously consider carefully what you require from the artist as an absolute minimum. You should specify how much work the artist will be expected to do, what kind of work it will be and what preparation you expect the artist to undertake. Secondly consider the rights you require in the contribution (the basic rights). It is perhaps obvious to say that you should try to obtain as many rights as you possibly can, even if you cannot obtain all-rights. Try to agree a contract that allows as much exploitation as possible without having to make further payment or seeking further permission. Many agents will offer to use a standard contract that they have drawn up themselves. If you accept this service you will have to check what rights you have acquired and if any options you have agreed have been included. It is best to provide your own contract that has been drawn up specifically for the current production. With this method there should be no misunderstandings. The standard contracts kept by agents often make no provision for uses that are out of the ordinary. Appendix A gives examples of contracts which you can use as templates.

The 1988 Copyright Act introduced a new concept into English law: moral rights. These are more fully explored in Chapter 10 but they do apply to certain spoken contributions. Any person speaking their own words, be they scripted or not, will have moral rights in their work if it is recorded in a material form, e.g. a sound or video recording. If you record and use this contribution without the contributor signing a moral rights waiver, the contributor can object to so-called 'derogatory' treatment. They have the right to be identified as the 'author' of the work. This may not appear to be a problem for your project but, should a contributor decide that they wish to object to anything you have done with their work, they may inhibit your continued use of the material until the matter is resolved. This resolution can be long and expensive, even if, in the end, the case is not proven. It is far wiser to take the simple step of adding a moral rights waiver to your contract in the beginning and asking all contributors to accept it.

7.4 MEMBERS OF THE PUBLIC

This group includes some quite eminent people but the bare bones of any contract offered to them are the same. It is important to be aware of exactly who it is that you wish to contract and to be aware of the importance of their contribution. If the contributor sees any advantage in the use you propose to make of their contribution then they are likely to prove amenable. If they do not care for the success of your project they do not have to co-operate.

Members of the public have rights in any contribution which they may make to your programme. They can be recorded without permission, but strictly speaking you cannot actually do anything with the recording without their permission. Therefore it is pretty pointless making the recording in the first place! Before making any recording with any member of the public, make sure that you have a form of contract or waiver that they can sign which grants you the rights you require in their contribution. Clarify the use you wish to make of the final programme/project and check that the contract or waiver covers at least this use, if not more. With members of the public you would be well advised to attempt to take all-rights in the contribution. Whatever you choose to do with the contribution you will not have to ask any further permission of the contributor.

There are some disadvantages to taking all-rights in a contribution and these need to be considered before making your final choice. If you have to pay your contributor, they might expect more money to compensate for the fact that you are taking all-rights. All-rights allows you to do anything and everything with the contribution but after weighing the costs of paying to get these broad rights you might prefer to be more specific. Secondly, you should try to be honest and respectful of your contributors' integrity and not mislead them regarding the use you will be making of their contribution. This is not simply in order to be a decent person (though that is no bad reason for taking care with other people's work) but it will also help you to retain goodwill. This is a vital element in making successful programmes.

It is not easy to decide how much to pay members of the public, if you pay them at all. You really have to assess what value you place on the contribution, and what money you have available to pay out. On the whole a nominal sum which shows your appreciation of their work is acceptable, but do establish that this is so before starting work. If you leave such discussions until after the recording takes place, then you open yourself up to being pushed into paying more than you can afford. Once again it is always wise to build options into your contract when you do not take all-rights. With this method you can agree in advance what amount of money or percentage of your income you will pay out to the contributors should you use the programme in ways other than those originally envisaged (see below). One issue which should be mentioned here is the possibility that a contributor will refuse you the right to exploit their work in the way you wish. When you are contracting an actor or a professional broadcaster it is not likely that they will refuse to grant you any rights – they will probably just want to argue about the money. However, a member of the public or someone who does not expect to earn their living from this sort of work may have a very different view on exploitation. Take a look at the following example. A producer was contracting artists for a video about Aids. Sufferers of the disease were contracted to be interviewed, but as the subject matter was so sensitive and the contributors did not wish money to be made out of their plight they restricted the use of their work to specific educational use only. They would not, under any circumstances, agree to any sale of the material and there is no way in which such permission can be forced.

In some cases contributors feel that they are no longer happy with what they said and what was recorded and they may decide that when the term of the contract they signed expires they will not grant permission for an extension to term. Sometimes, for example, academics or writers no longer wish for an old contribution to be used. They might have changed their mind about the subject or have said something since that is more up to date. They have the right to refuse this permission once the term of the licence has expired. You would be well advised, therefore, to plan ahead and try to ensure that you have the use of the material for as long as you need it.

7.5 ENGAGEMENT AND DRAWING UP CONTRACTS

If you decide that you do want to engage an actor or other person for your project, first choose your actor or performer! Where do you look? Most actors pay to have an entry in *Spotlight*, an expensive source of reference that runs to several volumes but it does help if you wish to select a certain type of actor by appearance and it also helps to put a name to a well-known face. *Spotlight*, which is also available on CD-ROM, can be acquired from 7 Leicester Place, London WC2H 7BP.

Some agents have videos of the artists (not just actors) on their books and these will give a greater impression of the skills of the performer. If you are still not sure which person to engage from a selection of artists, do hold an audition. If you have made your decision without an audition, try to speak directly to that person: persuade the actor that they want to work for you, and then negotiate an acceptable contract with them and with their agent. It is usually much easier to agree a contract with an artist or agent if the artist is already interested in the project.

Most actors have agents who will negotiate their fees and terms of employment. You need to issue a contract to the artist which sets out not only what work they will be doing for you and the fees they are to be paid for that work but also what rights you have acquired in their work. Be specific about what you are allowed to do with the recording. Your budget is likely to be limited, so do some sums before starting to talk money; then you will be better prepared against demands for more than you have offered. In some instances an actor or agent will say that they will not work for less than a specified amount. You do not have to accept this but whether you succeed in changing their minds will depend on your skills as a negotiator.

If you are planning to produce a large-scale drama you might decide to engage the services of a casting director. This professional will have an extensive knowledge of actors and their talents, and will help you to cast your programme or even take over the whole of the contracting arrangements. The services of a casting director can be expensive and might not be very economic. You can find some names in *Contacts* (obtainable from the same address as *Spotlight*) or you could ask Equity for the names of some reputable agencies.

Consider what you **must** be able to do with the contribution and also what else you would **like** to do with it. Once you have decided on use, then consider the fee you wish to pay. If you are producing a programme or product in or for an organization that has employed artists before and that therefore has a history of fees paid for similar work, let precedents guide your assessment of the fee but do not be hidebound by them. Try not to set a much higher or much lower fee than the norm; this would only create problems for you later.

After you have considered all these aspects, you can contact the artist or their agent. Only begin to negotiate the fee once you have engaged their interest in your project and let them have a full understanding of the work involved. When you do discuss the fee be prepared to take a bit of time.

It is wise to set yourself limits with regard to the amount of movement you will make in what you offer. Do not feel forced into reaching agreement during the initial conversation if your offer is not accepted straight away. Many agents and artists will want to think about the offer before reacting to it. This has the benefit that, once you have agreed the contract, you have a binding agreement. You want the artist to be committed to the work and not regretting their acceptance of it!

If you are asked to pay more, you can employ a variety of tactics. You could offer more money, if you can afford it, but do consider the implications of doing so:

● Will the fee agreed still be in line with your original assessment of what you should pay?
● What precedents are you setting?
● Will you be reducing your ability to pay proper amounts for other resources?

If you cannot increase the fee offer for whatever reason, it is possible to take the option of acquiring fewer up-front rights for the money. However, be careful to maintain the minimum level of rights clearance that you need. Try to include options in the contract which maintain the right to exploit the material as you desire but delay payment until the time that each additional right is exercised.

There are two ways of offering an all-rights contract to an artist. In the case of an important contributor to whom you are paying a considerable amount of money you might wish to provide a more elaborate contract than is strictly necessary. Of the two all-rights contracts given in Appendix A, the longer would be most appropriate in this instance. The shorter contract would be more appropriate for a short interview with a member of the public.

7.6 ROYALTIES V. RESIDUALS

Contributors to audio-visual programmes are paid a fee for taking part, and for certain rights. The rights not acquired in the initial payment are often available on payment of an additional amount. This can be calculated either as a percentage of the original fee (a **residual**) or as a percentage of the income derived from the additional rights being exploited (a **royalty**). Agents are often most interested in the amount of money their artist will receive immediately; however, if you only have limited funds available at the time of making the engagement but know (or hope) that there will be income later from further exploitation of the recording, it is worth trying to ensure that the right to exploit the actor's contribution is paid for out of your income derived from that exploitation. As with repeat fees, you can agree to pay out a residual or you can agree to pay out a royalty. But how do you decide which to use and try to get your actors to accept?

If you decide on residuals, you will always know how much money you must pay out in order to have the right to exploit the recording in a particular way. The disadvantage of this system is that your outgoings could exceed your income and therefore inhibit exploitation.

If you pay out only a percentage of your income, you will never have to pay out more than you earn – but do avoid the pitfalls. Be very careful that the amount of royalty paid out does not exceed the amount of income! If you offer everyone involved in your production 10% of the profits and you engage 11 people, you'll be paying out 110% of income. It is sensible to agree to pay the royalty as a percentage of profits and to agree that all contributors share a royalty amount, based on the relation of their initial fees. Take this example:

You engage five people to take part in your production: Joe Bloggs, Fred Smith, Jack Jones, Jill Jackson and Ruth Wright. Joe and Fred are paid £234 each, Jack and Jill are paid £141 each and Ruth is paid £250. You agree with them that they will all share in a royalty of 15% of your profits, the amount each receives being decided in the same way as their original fees relate to each other. This relationship is calculated in two steps:

1. Total the fees paid:
    £234 + £234 + £141 + £141 + £250 = £1000
2. For each individual, divide their original fee by this total and express the result as their percentage:
    £234 divided by £1000 represents 23.4%
    £141 divided by £1000 represents 14.1%
    £250 divided by £1000 represents 25%.

You sell the programme and at the end of the first accounting period your profit is £367. The royalty, at 15% of this profit, is therefore £55.05. Of this amount, Joe and Fred each get 23.4%, Jack and Jill each get 14.1% and Ruth gets 25%. Therefore you pay out two amounts of £12.88, two amounts of £7.76 and one amount of £13.77.

Try to be fair when defining profits. It is normal to deduct manufacturing and distribution costs, any residuals payable and any dealer discounts. If you also need to recoup all your production costs it will be a long time before any payments are made to contributors who are to be paid a royalty. In some instances royalty deals are made which agree to deduct the royalty from the income derived from the exploitation of the material. This means that the contributor will see some money once the programme is exploited to give rise to income. The decision over which route to take – residual or royalty, derived from income or profit – needs to be very carefully calculated. Sometimes artists will expect to receive an advance against royalty income. If your company is a small one you would probably wish to avoid this as it can prove expensive.

Do remember that if you engage artists on the basis of paying them a royalty derived from your income or profits derived from future exploitation, and the future exploitation does not live up to your expectations, you may lose some goodwill. When you use the same artists in any future work they might not prove so amenable. They might insist on being paid up front for all exploitation, or on a residual or on a higher royalty percentage.

7.7 THE EMPLOYMENT OF FOREIGN NATIONALS AND CHILDREN

7.7.1 FOREIGN NATIONALS

When engaging a foreign national, it is necessary to ensure that the artist can work in the UK. If you bring the artist to the UK from outside the EU you will have to apply for a work permit from the Department of Employment. This is no simple matter. You need to give sufficient reason for engaging the artist and not employing a British performer. This might include the provision of written evidence of their standing in their profession, and evidence of their 'uniqueness'. You will have to show what attempts you have made to employ an EU national in this role. You need to allow ample time for the application to be processed before the artist comes into the country – say, 6 weeks. You are by no means guaranteed the issue of a licence and there is no point in making the arrangements to bring in a foreign national without applying for a work permit. You will have to quote the fee being paid and give other personal details on the application.

If the artist is someone already working in the country with a work permit, then you must check that the work done for you is either covered by the work permit or that you are covered by an extension of that work permit. You will have to make provision for the payment of income tax. Artists who do not have double taxation agreements with the Inland Revenue must complete an income tax return.

7.7.2 CHILDREN

The employment of children (i.e. anyone under the age of 16) is subject to the strictures of the Education Act. This stipulates what sort of work children can undertake and the hours they may work. These vary depending on the age of the child. There is a limit to the number of days each child may work during the year, and you need to obtain, in most instances, a licence to employ a child. These are administered by the child's local education authority. This licence can take about 6 weeks to be issued. A child who attends stage school may work more days during term time than a child at an ordinary school. There is provision for children to work a limited number of unlicensed days per year (3 days per 6 calendar months). The unlicensed days must still comply with the law as regards hours etc. but you do not have the onerous business of applying for the licence. Employers of children are liable to be inspected by the Local Education Authority (the LEA) to ensure that they are working to the regulations. Children have to be chaperoned during attendance at work, starting from the time they leave home, until the time they return home, either by their parent or guardian or by a licensed chaperone or matron. The LEAs license chaperones and matrons, who may care for a maximum of 12 children at any one time. The children must remain with the chaperone at all times, so one chaperone for 12 children could prove impractical. Parents or guardians may only chaperone their own children, unless they are registered chaperones. Children employed to perform must also be tutored whilst they are away from school, so you might be required to engage the services of a tutor.

Children who act are not represented by Equity. Therefore their terms of employment, other than complying with the law, are not subject to any other agreement. You may negotiate their fee freely and take the rights you require, subject to the acceptance of the child and/or the parent or guardian. Their contracts must also be signed by the parent or guardian.

7.8 EMPLOYEES

The individuals employed to work on or in your production have rights in the work that they create unless, in the terms of their employment, those rights are assigned to the employer. (This does not refer to the employment of performers on an ad hoc basis.) If someone is employed, for example as a member of staff to produce copyright material, then as the Copyright Act states, the work produced 'during the course of employment' is the copyright of the employer, unless a contract is issued to the contrary. Thus if employees are engaged to work on the production of copyright material, you should be clear on the copyright position of the material they produce.

There is a second point to be made about 'employees' – but this is about someone else's employees, not yours. You might wish to interview someon about their job at the place of work. This interview requires an assignment of rights as discussed in section 7.4. In some cases the employer will say that the individual should not be paid a fee. This point is debatable but it is not our main concern here. You need to have a contract or waiver signed to ensure that you have adequate rights clearance. Some people will have been employed under such terms and conditions that their employer holds the copyright in any recorded interview that the person gives during their employment, but it would be unusual. It is more likely that the individual controls these rights, in which case the named individual ought to sign the contract and grant the rights required.

Film and footage

8

This chapter looks at the issues involved in using existing footage (film, video or audio tape) which has been recorded by a third party. Material such as this is often referred to as bought-in footage, or simply as footage. Under the 1988 Copyright Act films, sound recordings, broadcasts and cable transmissions are all protected by copyright, separately and independently from any copyright protection of their contents. Following EU copyright harmonization, protection runs for a period of 70 years from the end of the year in which the film was first released, or made (in the case of an unreleased film or sound recording). A broadcast or cable programme is protected for a period of 70 years from the end of the year of first transmission. The EU has changed the copyright position of films and television and radio programmes to bring their level of protection into line with that of other copyright works. Film brings with it the probability of having been created by the effort of several 'authors' (a term which includes the script writer, the director, the producer and the camera person) and copyright has been extended to run for 70 years after the death of the longest lived of those authors. Therefore a film made in the 1920s, which had gone out of copyright, has now come back into copyright and that right will persist into the twenty-first century.

The sections of the Copyright Act which allow for the free use of an insubstantial part of a copyright work apply to films, sound recordings, cable transmissions and to broadcasts. The right to use extracts for criticism and review or for the reporting of current events is allowed. One broadcaster's news and current affairs output can feature a clip recorded off-air from a sporting event for which a rival broadcaster may have exclusive transmission rights.

Some years ago *Washes Whiter*, a BBC series on advertising, featured many clips from historically significant advertisements without first clearing them, claiming free use under the allowance of fair dealing for the purposes of criticism and review. This attracted strong reaction from talent unions on behalf of their members but nevertheless remains a valid example of how this allowance may often be used in practice by programmes or series of a critical nature. It is a defence commonly used by broadcasters producing series on modern art. The drawback is that this part of UK law may not extend to all territories into which the broadcaster wishes to market. Denmark, for instance, has no fair dealing for the purposes of criticism or review and will be an excluded market for programmes or series making use of this clause in the UK act. What this leads to is that use may not be made of a substantial extract from a broadcast or a film in another production, without first seeking permission of the rights holder, except within the limits offered under the law of copyright.

8.1 ACQUIRING COMPLETE PROGRAMMES

There are two distinct ways of acquiring whole programmes: either by recording broadcasts off-the-air or by buying them on videotape or on film.

8.1.1 THE USE OF PROGRAMMES UNDER LICENSING SCHEMES

In the 1988 Copyright Act an 'educational establishment' (i.e. schools and colleges) may record broadcasts or cable transmissions free of charge off-the-air (i.e. by VCR) for the educational purposes of the institution, to the extent that no certified licensing scheme covering such recording is in operation. In practice this means that, unless the relevant rights holders offer a licensing scheme to schools and colleges, they have no means of preventing off-the-air recordings in schools and colleges. In the event the major broadcasters and other rights holders have set up a licensing scheme to enable them to derive income from educational establishments who wished to record broadcast programmes. This is the ERA (Educational Recording Agency) scheme. The ERA issues licences to educational establishments allowing them to record broadcasts for the purposes of educational instruction.

The Open University (OU) also operates a licensing scheme for recording their broadcast programmes off-the-air. This is run by the OU's marketing arm, Open University Educational Enterprises (OUEE). This scheme licenses educational institutions, training bodies and businesses to record OU programmes and use them for educational, instructional purposes.

The licences granted above only allow for licence holders to show the programmes recorded in a classroom setting, for 'educational purposes'. It does not allow for the programmes to be adapted, manipulated or edited, other than for the compilation of a tape of extracts of programmes recorded in this way. Neither may programmes recorded under the licensing schemes, whether in whole or in part, be included in any other programme. Off-the-air recordings can only be used by licence holders of the scheme(s) and not sold on or loaned to other users who are not licence holders. No additional acknowledgement is required when the programmes are recorded off-the-air. Any further use of programme material is subject to agreement with rights holders.

8.1.2 THE USE OF WHOLE PROGRAMMES OUTSIDE THE LICENSING SCHEMES

It is of course possible for individuals and organizations to buy copies of programmes and films for use in a variety of ways. Everyone will be familiar with the sale of films and broadcast programmes on cassette through high street shops and mail order. For such programmes the buyer is generally licensed to use them for private viewing purposes only. Further clearance is essential if the buyer wishes to use the programmes for other purposes. It is likely that the licensee may be required to buy the programme again from a different source.

This use is often called home video or home audio sale, and the rights which need to be cleared with rights holders in any specific programme are called home video rights or home audio rights. Rights holders frequently levy their fees in the form of a royalty for this permission, which means that they receive a proportion of the retail price from each sale. This right is different from that which is cleared when offering films or programmes for hire. Programmes and films sold to companies for the specific purpose of rental have been cleared for that purpose, and consequently cost more to buy than do home retail versions of the same programme.

Many producers of programmes and films sell their programmes for uses other than for private viewing or for rental for private viewing. The most common, other than for broadcast, is for showing to non-paying audiences. This allows for the programmes to be screened for teaching and training purposes in a classroom environment or for showing for entertainment, for example in a club or other group gathering. The physical situation is less important than is the fact that the audience must not be charged an admission fee in order to view the programme. The right to show to non-paying audiences is separate from the right to sell for private viewing purposes. The right to show to non-paying audiences is frequently called the non-theatric right and again normally requires a fee to be paid to rights holders. This right does not allow for the showing of the programme to paying audiences in a cinematic or theatric setting. This right, the theatric right, is normally only cleared in programmes which are destined for cinema release. Finding films and programmes available for sale outside the retail market can be hard work. If the programme and producer are identifiable, the starting point of the search is made by approaching the producer or broadcaster. If the programme is not identifiable, there are various ways of looking, though none is exhaustive. The British Film Institute's National Film and Television

Archive holds a national archive of British film and television at their site in Berkhampsted, Hertfordshire. The prime function of this collection is to preserve material but access to the collection is possible and copies of programmes are available for sale in certain instances. Remember, though, that even if the BFI collection does contain a copy of the programme you are seeking, it is likely that the rights holder will also have to be approached for a licence. Nevertheless, the collection can be of great use to researchers. Another useful source for information is the *British National Film and Video Catalogue* (BNFVC) produced by the BFI. This is a quarterly publication, with an annual cumulation. It lists films and programmes available for sale or non-theatric hire. Film and video producers operating in the educational sector have a wonderful resource open to them through the British Universities Film and Video Council (BUFVC). The BUFVC produces a variety of publications to help in the use of audio-visual material in education. *Film and Television Collections in Europe: the MAP-TV Guide* (published by Blueprint, 1995) lists audio-visual collections and is the definitive guide to sourcing film and footage.

8.1.3 THE USE OF ADVERTISEMENTS

Film and television advertisements are protected by copyright in the same way as other films or programmes. Although the series mentioned earlier did use them without clearance, most other uses would probably fall outside the defence available in that instance.

Using advertising material involves obtaining clearance from the advertising agency as copyright owner of the material. It might not always be clear who the agency was, but a good starting point is to contact the company whose products are being advertised. Occasionally the agency or the company commissioning the advertisement will be wary of allowing the work to be used, but in many cases they are only too happy to receive additional exposure and will license the material at little or no charge. If you are making critical remarks about the product or the advertisement you might find the rights more difficult to clear, but frequently companies see any use of their advertisements as being publicity worth having. In any event, the fact that the advertisement is to be subjected to critical commentary may be sufficient to provide for its use under the defence of fair dealing for the purposes of criticism or review.

Once use of the advertisement has been cleared with the production company, the next step is to clear the rights of the artists involved – actors, musicians, etc. If they are actors (which is likely) they will expect to receive Equity rates (Chapter 7). If the advertisement contains music it may have to be cleared for re-use in another project (Chapter 6).

8.2 THE USE OF EXTRACTS FROM FILMS AND PROGRAMMES

The use of extracts from films and programmes is often simply referred to as the use of footage. Unless a production company or organization controls the rights to a large back catalogue of production material, it is unlikely to have easy access to footage. Where does it go to find stock material or information about it? Once the source of such material has been traced, how is it accessed and how is it cleared for exploitation in another production? This section looks at all these issues in turn.

8.2.1 SOURCES OF FOOTAGE

Appendix B lists sources and their contact numbers for easy reference. Broadcasters and production companies have a vast collection of programmes that have been produced and broadcast over the years. The BBC has a specific department, Film Library Sales, responsible for marketing footage. This department can locate material and issue a licence to cover its use. A rate card is used to determine the price according to categories of use. For use of material from any of the ITV companies, approach the individual company rather than a central clearance library. The independent television companies each have their various specializations and offer a varied selection of material (some more than others). Again, the companies operate a rate card.

For other material it is worth taking into account the subject matter being researched and considering other organizations that might control useful material. Many industries and businesses produce films and videos which may be available for use at a price. For example, if the subject area is the processes involved in sugar production a good place to start could be with the major sugar companies such as British Sugar plc or Tate & Lyle. Approach the publicity departments in the first instance. University departments, research organizations and institutions often have film or video collections produced in the course of their work. As long as the research is not strictly secret and confidential, access may be possible. For commercial film material, approach the major distributors or production companies for both access and clearance. The usual distributors have a rate card detailing the charges made for specific use.

Then there are the collections of news-style footage. British Movietone and British Pathé News have marvellous collections of cinema newsreels that give a wonderful vision of the British life and history during the early twentieth century. They are widely used in documentary and historical programmes and are available (at a price) for most uses. Visnews and Reuters are modern news-gathering companies and can provide news material from vast collections dating from 1896. The material has been shot from around the world, but again is available at a price.

These companies are far from being the only sources of material. For a more comprehensive list consult the Federation of Commercial Audio-visual Libraries (FOCAL). FOCAL is the trade association of the film libraries; it also represents film researchers. It can help with lists of members, it runs seminars and it produces a regular journal. Finally there are some agencies who search out film footage for clients. If producers are unable or unwilling to attempt to search out material themselves and can afford to stretch the budget, these agencies can prove invaluable.

8.2.2 CHOOSING THE FOOTAGE YOU WANT TO USE

A great deal of time can be spent in searching for companies holding the material you want to use, but additional time must then be spent in selecting the most appropriate footage for the production. It is quite acceptable to request a viewing copy of the programmes but you should expect to pay for the service. The production of viewing copies is a costly process. Old films and programmes were recorded on a different format than is commonly used today, and the transfer to VHS or other modern formats is often difficult and time consuming and so it may not be cost effective to provide viewing copies. Old nitrate film is highly flammable and dangerous to handle. Part of the job of the National Film and Television Archive is to preserve this material and to copy it on to a modern format. If the material being sought is on an old format, getting access to it may be either extremely difficult or impossible and some organizations will insist that material may only be viewed on their premises. The owners of the films or programmes may feel that the provision of video copies is an invitation to copy without gaining proper clearance.

In order to be on the safe side, a sensible option is to have a choice of material from which to select, unless it is certain at the outset that the footage can be cleared for the use in mind, and at an acceptable price.

8.2.3 CLEARING THE MATERIAL

Once the footage, or a range of footage, has been selected the rights holder must be approached for copyright clearance. Unless they have provided clearance details at the time of choosing the material, contact the rights holder by phone to start the ball rolling. The rights holder will often be able to quote a price straight away if the proposed use is straightforward, but if the proposal is rather more unusual they may not. There is no need to accept the price quoted if it appears too high: always attempt to negotiate. Remember that unless the licensee is prepared to say no to the film company or rights holder, they may be forced to pay the price quoted – but do try. It can be very worthwhile to negotiate, and with many of the prices quoted for the use of footage amounting to thousands of pounds, there is an incentive to bargain.

If the price is too high for the production budget, it might be possible to pay only for an initial level exploitation. Options on extra uses can then be built into the licence, payable only as exercised. This means that you agree that use of the material in other ways is agreed and guaranteed under licence, but only paid for as and when the additional rights are exercised. If options are granted, ensure that the price is clear. Sometimes the prices quoted for additional rights have only a limited life, particularly if they are taken from a rate card. These rates normally rise annually, and if a licensee goes back after the rate rise the rights holder will often expect to charge the rate then current.

Once initial contact has been made, a written follow-up is often essential. Then, when the price has been agreed (perhaps after protracted negotiations), the licence must be signed. Many broadcasters, producers, film companies and libraries operate to standard licences. Before signing these make sure that the licence allows for the the material to be used as agreed. Other rights holders might only issue an invoice. This is not necessarily wrong, but unless there is either written evidence of the rights acquired or the invoice itself specifies the grant of rights, the practice may open up problems later.

Even when the rights in the footage have been cleared with the production company or rights holder, some underlying rights may remain to be cleared – for example, those of the contributors or of the music. If actors are involved, expect to pay Equity rates. If there is music in the clip, the rights in that may also have to be cleared. Be aware of any other copyright material contained in the extract and check whether any other rights need to be accounted for. If the footage source advises that there are no further rights to clear, ensure that there is a warranty within the contract or licence which will provide adequate cover in the event of a claim being made.

This is probably the right time to look at a couple of salutary cases of film clearances that were far from smooth. A well-known production company was involved in a co-production with another equally well-known institution in producing a teaching pack (including film and audio and text) on media studies. Obviously a pack of this sort would need to include footage acquired from commercial sources. The programmes were produced and the pack designed using a still photograph from one piece of footage as the cover picture for the accompanying textbook and for the wrap-around pack itself. It was agreed that the pack would be sold through retail outlets and direct to schools. It was only once production was complete and the clearances checked prior to release that two problems regarding footage were first identified.

Firstly the still photograph had been taken from footage cleared only for use in the pack videocassette. Clearance did not cover its use as a still picture on the book or on the wrap-around pack. Furthermore, the material origi-nated in Italy so an approach had to be made to the Italian production company to clear the material for use as a still photograph. This proved diffi-cult and protracted. Finally the production company insisted that the contrib-utor who appeared in the still photograph had to be consulted, as she had not granted this type of clearance to them. The contributor was French and a minor, adding further complications of language, commercial expectations and parental consent. Clearance was eventually negotiated at a cost of £1000 simply for the use of the photograph. As the programme had been completed and the books already printed, even this was cheaper than having to reprint the material – but it was still much, much more than would have been paid had clearance been negotiated at an earlier stage in production.

The second problem with this pack involved a short piece of footage taken from a well known American animated cartoon. The original clearance gained was straight forward but not quite adequate: it did not allow for the sale of the material through retail shops. When this omission was identified, the cartoon producer was again approached to extend the original clearance. By then, the American cartoon company had been taken over by a very large media conglomerate, which had introduced a policy of no longer licensing this material for any purpose at any price. The programme had to be re-edited and the footage removed before retail sales were possible. The animated cartoon has since been adapted and released as a full-length Hollywood feature film using a combination of live actors and computer animation.

The amounts of money paid for the clearance of footage are probably the highest copyright fees paid. Some clearances of comparatively short segments of footage (under 2 minutes) can cost over £10 000 for a 5-year licence simply for the right to sell the material (i.e. excluding any other exploitation rights). Calculations are made and rates charged based on a few standard criteria. Some companies charge per second, some per minute or part thereof, and some by the foot or metre of film used. They will often make a minimum charge, e.g. 30 seconds' worth or a specific minimum licensing fee. The use of a good variety of authentic footage can often really lift a programme to a new level, but producers must be aware of the cost and rights position before including a mass of third party footage in a programme.

8.3. THE USE OF EXISTING SOUND MATERIAL

Chapter 6 looks at the use of music and in one particular at the use of commercial recordings. This section looks at the use of any other recorded sounds – radio programmes and records or tapes or discs of readings, plays, talks and lectures, to name a few.

8.3.1 THE USE OF RADIO PROGRAMMES

With the introduction of local and national commercial radio stations to compete with established BBC stations, and with the establishment of a commercial, independent production industry serving both sectors, there is now a choice of radio programming produced by any number of producers. In clearing such material, the easiest first approach is to the broadcaster. The broadcaster may not be the rights holder but will be able either to contact the rights holder or to pass on a contact name. The situation is less organized and easy for producers simply seeking sound material. Try approaching the BBC or one of the other broadcasters if you know they are likely to have relevant material. Another source is the Association of Independent Radio Companies (the trade association for independent broadcasters).

Once the material has been located, how is it cleared? The radio industry is not quite so responsive to sales and licensing opportunities for the exploitation of sound-only recorded materials as are some other media industries. The BBC may now sell radio programmes on audio cassette and has distributed radio material throughout the world for use by overseas radio stations for many years, but it does not have a dedicated department for the sale of extracts of radio programming in the way that it does for the sale of television material. For non-BBC material, approach the producers or broadcasters who might (but more probably might not) have a structure for dealing with your enquiry or requirements. Persevere until they answer.

Obtaining a licence to use the material is essential before using a substantial amount in another programme or in some other form of exploitation. Check that the material is available for use where, how and for as long as is needed. It is probable that licensees will be expected to draw up the licence themselves, though some producers may wish to do so; either way check it carefully, as with all licences. The broadcaster or producer may grant permission to use the recording but, again, the rights in the material contained within it might not be cleared as part of the licensing agreement, i.e. the contributors or the music. Always check the position of these items and re-clear if necessary.

8.3.2 THE USE OF OTHER SOUND MATERIAL

Other sound material includes sound recording of non-musical material, such as readings, plays, talks or lectures. It is difficult to advise on how to find this type of material, except to emphasize that the best place to begin a search is by contacting companies, organizations or educational institutions that have a commercial or educational interest in the area the producer wishes to explore. When seeking privately recorded material try advertising in the press, or make use of local societies focusing on special interest groups – local historical societies and the like. Once the material is identified, permission covering the proposed use must be obtained, just as for any commercially controlled material. The rights holder must agree the use, and may have to re-clear some of the content before licensing. If the recording was made for private and research purposes it is unlikely that any clearances were made, but this subsequent use may require that they are. Even if the rights holder is not aware of that fact, the producer should be and should seek to clear any material as appropriate. The fact that material does not need clearance for private use does not allow for subsequent use without further clearance.

Here is an example of the clearances required for the use of a sound recording:

A producer found a recording of John Betjeman reading some of his poetry to a musical accompaniment. He wished to include this in his programme, which was destined for teaching students at the Open University and for non-theatric sale to other teaching organizations. In order to clear the material for this use an approach was made to the owner of the recording for permission to use it, and a fee was paid. Permission did not cover any of the rights of the contributors or content. Further approaches then had to be made to the Betjeman estate and two further fees paid – one for the use of the poem, which was handled by one agent, and one for the recording by Betjeman himself, handled by another agent and subject to a separate contract. Then an approach had to be made to MCPS for the clearance of the music and an approach to the performer for the use of his performance.

Clearing sound material

1. *Has the rights owner in the sound recording cleared all rights within the material?*
2. *Are you required to clear the content of the material?*
   Does the material include any people?
   Does the material include any recorded music?
   Does the material include any live music?
   Does the material include any written material?
   Does the material include any other bought-in material?

Software

9

For multimedia producers, software is the engine that drives the production and delivers it to the user audience. It fulfils the same function that transmitters and a broadcast system does for television producers. Without controlling access and distribution rights to software, multimedia producers are denied access to their targeted audience. This chapter is intended to provide an extended checklist of common concerns and the provision of adequate safeguards in using proprietary packages and commissioned software. More than any other media category, software licensing is subject to individual and sometimes idiosyncratic licensing agreements that vary widely from case to case. The golden rule is to read each licence carefully, not expecting each to follow a common pattern set by others.

Software is treated as a literary work under UK copyright legislation but computer-generated work does not carry the moral rights protection offered to other literary works. However, accompanying wrap-around or instructional literature, such as user manuals, will be covered by moral rights and should be used accordingly. While this will not be a problem for works created by employees in the course of their employment, it might be a consideration for producers to bear in mind when commissioning independent contractors or self-employed authors. In such circumstances a moral rights waiver is an important part of the commissioning contract.

The identification and development of a comprehensive user specification is an essential first step to either commissioning a bespoke authored package or licensing proprietary software. Briefly, the producer should identify the functionality of the package (what is it meant to do), the volume of data it is to hold and carry and the number of people who need access. There must also be an analysis of the expected growth of the project to give an indication of how growth, volumes and user access might change over time. These combine to create a requirement specification against which commissioned authors may tender and proprietary packages may be measured. Producers embarking upon this exercise for the first time could be well advised to contact an independent consultant for advice, or at least to contract the assistance of a more experienced colleague.

9.1 COMMISSIONED SOFTWARE

While the creation of a requirement specification is essential in defining both commissioned and proprietary packages, some considerations apply more closely to the commissioning of software in particular. It is important that the contract, as with any other commissioning contract, should specify who owns copyright and other rights in the commissioned work and any enhancements which may be developed or implemented subsequently. It is common practice under some standard software licensing arrangements for enhancements to the package to be deemed the copyright of the originating commissioned author or developer, even if those enhancements have been developed and implemented entirely by the user. The practice is something that multimedia producers should avoid wherever possible. In fact, some agreements do not allow users to enhance the package, tying them instead to a continuing relationship with the author or developer for future ongoing developments to the package as the system evolves. A commissioning contract should specify who is authorized to develop or implement enhancements and tie up the details. Even if producers think they may not make use of the right to produce their own enhancements, the contract should allow for the possibility for them either to implement their own work or to commission enhancements from other agencies as the commissioning producer deems necessary.

9.2 INTELLECTUAL PROPERTY RIGHTS

Whether considering commissioned or proprietary software packages, producers should run the following checklist of intellectual property provisions which should be covered by all contracts. The first applies to proprietary packages and is fundamental to their use. It is that commercial packages are not bought by the user: they are only licensed. This is essential to the understanding of how such packages work and the restrictions which developers may, through licensing, place upon users. It is a common misunderstanding for licensed users to imagine that money changing hands means that they have bought the commercial package and may use it how they please, without having to read the licence. In fact, commercial software packages are made available under licence and the nature of the licence determines how they may be used. This applies equally to software tools, such as GIF and other artwork packages used in developing multimedia packages, and to bigger, more readily apparent licensed software, such as database packages. The multimedia producer must be alert to the fact that in selecting or commissioning a software package, or using a software tool in developing or accessing artwork, for example, the rights implications of making the selection must be considered just as they are when selecting text, footage, performers or any of the other more overt elements of a production. Out of sight can, so often, be out of mind.

Software licences

Being aware that the proprietary software is licensed and thus subject to restrictions, the producer should check each licence against the following list:

- *Does the licence impose a limitation of use to identified equipment and for the licensee's own data only?*
- *Is the loaning, subletting or transference of the package restricted or proscribed?*
- *Does the licence impose a responsibility on the licensee to observe levels of security or confidence? What are the penalties for breach?*
- *Are restrictions imposed on the adaptation or decompilation of the software?*
- *What provision is made for the termination of the licence? Does the licence terminate at the expiry of a specified period; or in the case of either party breaching the agreement; or in the case of insolvency; or in the case of control of the licensee's company changing hands; or upon the sale of the business; or upon the sale of the computers to which the licences apply? All of these, singly or in combination, may apply.*

Licensees should also check if the licence agreement includes warranties and support provision sufficient for their needs. Access to the source code for maintenance purposes should also be negotiated wherever possible and inserted in the contract, together with an agreed level of charges relating to technical and training support.

In most licensing agreements, the supplier has the advantage of prior knowledge. Like many other software users, multimedia producers are often new to the licensing culture of the software industry and are often presented with a standard licensing agreement prepared and ready for signature or, worse still, are asked to accept that the terms of a shrink-wrap licence are valid. Producers would be wise to take the initiative by being active in leading negotiation on those areas of the contract in which they have prior experience. Price negotiation is a good starting point, as are details of the function the software is expected to perform. Producers may not be fluent in the technical argot of software engineering but they will know and understand the function in a lay person's terms. Raise concerns about the nature of the licence as early as possible, either because it is indistinct or expressed in terms that are unfamiliar or simply because it is unacceptable. Make provision for the supplier to compensate for the user's lack of expertise or familiarity by supplying training and error correction support, a telephone hotline for on-line support and fault diagnosis and continuing guaranteed support for the life of the licence, particularly in respect of enhancements to maintain the software's suitability as the user's needs grow. As with any other supplier or contracted author, of course, software developers and providers should be assessed for their experience in providing packages of the type under consideration, for their reputation among existing customers and currently live projects and for their technical expertise in the area. Other factors to be considered include geographical location (whether they are close enough to offer a truly accessible service) and financial and managerial stability.

9.3 INDEMNITY

The licensee's liability should be limited in the case of alleged infringement of copyright, patents or trade marks by a third party. Employers should also seek to limit their liability for infringement of trade secrets by an employee. To safeguard their own position in case of software being withdrawn, producers (in their role of product supplier) should also reserve their right to terminate a licence, to use the production in a specific software application and to replace any infringing software with software performing similar functions. This limits the effect of claims for infringement and possible claims from licensed users of the production and is particularly useful in cases where producers anticipate co-production deals or marketing.

9.4 MARKETING

The question of marketing raises other questions in respect of computer-driven productions. They represent both sides of the licensor/licensee divide and may usefully be used by either party. Licences may be limited by quantity, by geographical sales territory or by time and licensors will seek to retain their right to renew or extend their licences only if the initial sales returns are satisfactory. The right to cancel licences should the product not appear on the market, or not be marketed with sufficient vigour, may also be retained. Software licences often run for a term of 5 years. They should be tightly drafted to define the form in which the material will be produced and, if relevant, the hardware platform on which it is intended to run. Royalty rates vary widely, ranging from 7% to 30% of net receipts according to the value of the data being carried. Copyright notices should be displayed on screen together with accompanying identifying text giving fuller details of the marketing and development company.

9.5 KEY CONTRACT TERMS

9.5.1 CONSIDERATION

As in all contracts, some consideration in money or in kind should be exchanged in order to validate the contract.

9.5.2 CONDITIONS

Breach of a defined condition will give the injured party an option to treat the contract as being terminated and claim a right to damages. If a condition is breached and the injured party chooses not to exercise their right to terminate the contract, the contract is affirmed as being still in force. The injured party then cannot use this same breach of conditions to terminate the contract at a later date. This does not, however, affect their ability to retain and later exercise their right to claim damages for breach. It is important for multimedia producers that the contract should include a condition that the software will be suitable for their users' requirements – for example, it must be able to run on specified hardware, even if supplied by another source. If the 'fit for use' question is not addressed in the contract, it might still be possible for the user to act on the grounds that the software provider or developer misrepresented their product, but it is simpler and tidier to have the matter addressed formally in the contract. The contract should guarantee that the software can run successfully on current or proposed equipment.

9.5.3 SOURCE CODE

In order to ensure the licensee's continuing ability to update, develop and use the program in the event of the licensor ceasing to exist or to trade, it is common practice for licensing agreements to make provision for the depositing of a complete copy of the source code either with a mutually agreeable third party or with the licensee. The deposit should include any other utility code or data or other resource used to build the executable software from the source code. It should be updated regularly so as to keep pace with the software package itself as it is distributed or used in updated versions by the licensee. The practice ensures that in the event of the licensor ceasing to trade or going out of existence, the licensee will continue to have access to that part of the package (the source code) necessary to maintain the ability to update and develop the software as necessary.

9.5.4 WARRANTY

Breach of warranty will give the injured party a right to claim damages in respect of relatively minor faults.

Producers contracting for the development or supply of software may find that incorporating conditions in the contract is an effective way of calling upon remedies for breach of contract or of allowing for discharging the contract and either withholding payment or reclaiming payment. Whether the supply of software is determined to be a supply of goods or a supply of services can vary according to circumstances. Commissioned packages written entirely to specification are likely to be treated as being the supply of services, and off-the-shelf proprietary packages as the provision of goods.

9.6 INFRINGEMENT OF SOFTWARE

As software is treated as a literary work under UK legislation, many of the concepts of infringement may be carried forward from an understanding of infringement as applied to literary works. The translation of software from one language to another, for example, is analogous to the translation of a novel from English into French. Both acts of translation infringe copyright in the original unless done with permission. In the case of a computer program the act of translation includes a version of the program in which it is converted into or out of a computer language or code or into a different computer language or code. It does not include the strictly incidental translation from one code into or out of another that may take place in the normal running of the program.

Other infringing acts include the possession or use of infringing copies of software. By this is meant the use of pirated copies of software – something which is readily understood and avoided by most reasonable users – and also unlicensed software, of which many users are less aware or regard as being somehow less important. Copyright is infringed by anyone possessing or using infringing (unlicensed) software in the following ways, if they know or have reason to believe that the copy is an infringing copy:

- possession in the course of business;
- selling or hiring;
- exhibiting in public or distributing;
- distributing in any way so as to affect prejudicially the copyright owner.

Interestingly for academic and research users of software, there is no provision for the fair use of software for the purpose of research or private study as there is for other literary works.

Copyright is also infringed by the manufacture, possession, sale or importation of any article specifically designed or adapted for making copies of infringing software. Lawful users may make back-up copies of programs without infringing, provided that the copies are necessary to achieve the lawful user's right to use the program.

For multimedia producers interested in exploring the possibilities of networked systems and Internet or cable distribution, the most likely potential for inadvertent infringement is carried by the transmission of unlicensed software knowing, or having reason to believe, that infringing copies of the work will be made.

This all points to the importance of producers assessing their distribution and marketing plans realistically and licensing their software accordingly. Restrictions imposed by licensing will fundamentally affect their ability to exploit productions to their full potential, unless licensing is undertaken with care. Three particular areas are frequently overlooked: decompilation, runtime rights and authoring tools.

9.6.1 DECOMPILATION

Decompilation is a frequently used and frequently misunderstood term referring to the process of reproducing or translating a computer program's machine-readable code in order to allow for the analysis of the program in a human-readable source code. It is achieved by loading a program's object code (the machine-readable code) into a computer and running it with decompilation software in order to produce or expose the source code (human-readable code). Put simply, it takes the software apart in order to see how it works. A user's ability to decompile legitimately depends upon their satisfying two key requirements: decompilation must be for a legitimate purpose and the user must be a lawful user. The legitimate purpose (the permitted objective) of decompilation is defined in the Copyright (Computer Programs) Regulations 1992 as obtaining 'information necessary to create an independent program which can be operated with the program decompiled or with an other program'. A lawful user is simply a person who (whether under a licence to do any acts restricted by the copyright in the program or otherwise) has a right to use the program. Sections 50A and 50B of the Regulations refer specifically to decompilation.

The information obtained by decompilation must not be used for any purpose other than the permitted objective. Decompilation cannot be undertaken if the information is available to the user by other means, for instance via the supplier or program developer. Such access is often achieved as part of the licensing agreement. Legitimate decompilation is generally undertaken in order to ensure that the software being decompiled will work effectively with other packages (often referred to as interoperability). It cannot be prohibited in licensing contracts with lawful users, though some software providers attempt to do so. It does present a threat to software developers as a possible means of rivals gaining privileged trade information about the construction of the program and in normal circumstances, not involving a lawful user or not undertaken for legitimate purposes, decompilation clearly infringes copyright as an unauthorized copying and adaptation of the work.

The UK's implementation of the EU Software Directive in January 1993 allows for the reverse engineering (decompilation) of a program in order to ensure that it can operate in an existing environment. This is different from decompiling simply in order to find out how a program goes about doing its work, which is not permitted. (A user cannot decompile in order to create a program which is similar in expression to the program which is being decompiled.) The act of decompilation must be directly related to the implementation of practical working coincidence between programs interacting or running simultaneously or in some way interdependent upon each other for the effective running of the application. Its legitimacy depends upon the interaction of a number of factors: the purpose and intended use of the decompilation, the nature of the copyright work being decompiled, the amount of copying involved and, importantly, the extent to which it may affect the market potential of the original work. Some licensing agreements specify how and why licensees may decompile the program while others, as we have said, specifically attempt to deny users' rights to decompile.

9.6.2 RUNTIME RIGHTS

This commonly used term does not have a clear definition but generally is taken to mean the right to distribute reduced or extracted versions of authoring systems along with the application built by using them. This allows end users to operate the application (the CD-ROM, for instance) without needing to install the full authoring system on their computer. Some multimedia authoring tools permit the free distribution of runtime versions of the system to permit end users to operate programs built with the system. Others allow for such use only under licence, on payment of specified royalties audited back through the multimedia producer. Still more may restrict the producer's ability to license runtime rights at all, preferring to take the opportunity to force end users to buy the complete package, though this is not common. Producers must operate within the terms of the licence under which they use authoring tools.

9.6.3 AUTHORING TOOLS

Other licensing considerations to take into account when using commercially produced authoring tools include limitations on the use of mapping programs and GIFs (software tools used to compress and capture visual information for CD and other digitized formats). Mapping programs designed to create map artwork often carry the restriction that while they may be used freely to create individual maps within a largely text-based production (to illustrate a history book, for example) they may not be used to create an atlas without further licences being negotiated. GIFs may be similarly restricted by licensing agreements that are often overlooked by users. Some recent licensing arrangements have specified royalty returns to the software developer for each use of a product developed using GIF software. The lesson is that software licensing often reaches areas that conventional publishing or broadcasting licence agreements take for granted as being part of the functionality bought with supply of the package. Multimedia producers coming from an environment outside computing are often unaware of the extent to which their production work may be confined by software licensing agreements and may find that they are in breach of licensing agreements or are committed to payments that were not taken into account when the project was in production.

9.7 LICENSING

What type of licence is appropriate to your needs? Most licences fall into one of three categories: single-user, multi-user and site.

9.7.1 SINGLE-USER LICENCES

Single-user licences do not permit loading of the software on to networked systems for simultaneous access by more than one user. They licence per user and software is installed separately on each machine.

9.7.2 MULTI-USER LICENCES

Multi-user licences give the licensee the right for a number of users to access and use the software simultaneously. The software is accessed via a Local Area Network (LAN) by means of a software package or a CD-ROM being loaded and distributed through the network. The benefit of multi-user licensing agreements is that, being licensed according to user numbers rather than location, they allow for access by users off-site or on the move. Multimedia producers intending to license their product for networked use must ensure that they have the necessary software licensing in place before making the product available.

9.7.3 SITE LICENCES

Site licences are more restrictive geographically. They do not permit users to access systems at home or on the move and can sometimes be comparatively expensive. As a site licence refers to a specific site, institutional users (for instance) may need to have a licence for each of their sites, unless they can define 'site' as equivalent to 'institution' in the licence.

9.8 BULLETIN BOARDS AND ONLINE SERVICES

Software downloaded from bulletin boards and on-line information services such as Compuserve, or programs and utilities available through free distribution via magazines and journal cover disks and CDs, are commonly combined under the headings of shareware and public domain software. These are often confusingly understood to be freely available for use in all formats, for all purposes. In fact, though public domain software may be passed to friends and colleagues without permission, it is often on the understanding that the use is not for commercial gain. In the increasingly blurred lines that divide education, research and entrepreneurial activity, it is sometimes difficult to establish what is for commercial gain and what is not.

Shareware, a term often wrongly used as being synonymous with public domain software, is actually used under licence. Use is determined by the author's message (in effect the licence) displayed by the act of accessing the program. Often shareware may be passed on subject to paying a small levy. Sometimes further use depends upon obtaining the author's permission. Magazine and journal cover disks and CDs may fall under either category and should be treated accordingly.

Not all material is so easily defined, particularly accessed systems and bulletin boards. Further use is dependent upon contacting the copyright owner for permission. For example, the network access facility Compuserve has produced a policy document to guide its members for use of material under the compilation licence exercised by Compuserve under US copyright. Compuserve collects data, adds value to it and then licenses it on to others. This does not mean it holds copyright on all the individual pieces of information held within it. All copyright, with the exception of public domain elements, resides with individual authors. Rules covering access are strict. Breaking them can result in exclusion from the service or in legal action. Copyright material, including shareware, cannot be loaded on to the system without the author's permission. Public domain software may be loaded and used by anyone.

In order to clear and license shareware legitimately users must comply with the licensing instructions presented on screen as part of the shareware package, usually as the front page displayed upon the program being accessed. Licensing rates may vary according to use. Many shareware providers impose no charge for personal or educational (non-profit) use of their material. Other fees may range from sending or electronically transferring a few dollars to the author's account, through to a full royalties-based licensing agreement.

Moral rights 10

Some producers, coming from the UK/US tradition, approach the concept of moral rights, or droit moral, with apprehension. They have the vague feelings of unease of someone with a grumbling appendix. They know it is there, but are not sure why it is there, what function it serves or how they are likely to benefit from the pain. All they know is that at some point the thing is likely to go critical. These feelings come out of the differing approaches to copyright that the two traditions bring to the author's relationship with the work. Briefly, for the Anglo-Saxon tradition, copyright is a commercial property right to be bought and sold, while for the civil law traditions of other European countries, such as France, and others elsewhere such as Japan, the author's rights are integrally bound up with a continuing interest in the work in the way that a parent is seen to have a continuing interest in the progress of a child. It is the author's continuing interest in the work which is protected by moral rights: they are separate from copyright, are personal to the author or the author's estate, and can be handed down.

In countries where moral rights have traditionally been developed and respected, they are held to be separate from copyright, at least in the sense that while copyright as a commercial transaction may be sold by the author, moral rights are inalienable and continue to operate even if copyright in a work has passed to another. Moral rights allow for the author to maintain a continuing control over the ways in which the work is used, so as to maintain the integrity of both the work and the author's reputation and artistic sensibility. They do not expire on the author's death but are inherited by the estate. They protect the author's right to object to derogatory treatment of the work and to be named as author. They may also ensure a right of equitable remuneration which provides for an author to re-negotiate fair returns on early works subsequent to a later work becoming a commercial success.

In order to comply with the Berne Convention, of which the UK is an adherent, the Copyright, Designs and Patents Act 1988 introduced some vestigial form of moral rights into UK legislation. It did so in a way which those used to established droit moral traditions would see as grudging. Only two rights were introduced: the right to be named as author and the right to object to derogatory treatment of the work. The right to be named as author does not become operable until asserted in writing. Neither of these rights may be bought or sold. Therefore an author who assigns copyright in a work to another person or organization cannot assign the moral rights.

Many UK publishers and broadcasters absorbed the changes embodied in the newly introduced rights by requiring both authors and performers to waive them. This means that the rights holder cannot object to derogatory treatment or insist on being named as the 'author' of the work. Publishers and producers wish for authors and other rights holders to waive their moral rights in order to have a free hand when editing and adapting material. They feel that this free hand is essential when considering the time and money they invest in projects. They do, however, find that they are hard pressed to persuade some people to waive rights, and they then have to accept either that the work is not available to them or that they must agree any alterations with the rights holder. Depending on who the rights holder is will dictate whether or not this task is easy. Interestingly, this often has the effect of reinforcing protection already offered to high status artists under contractual provision. New and emerging authors and artists are often unable, from a comparatively weak bargaining position, to resist the pressure to waive their moral rights, while those who are established and, significantly, bring returns in terms of either prestige or income are better placed.

10.1 RIGHT OF IDENTIFICATION (PATERNITY RIGHT)

The author's right to be identified as author (creator) of the work or the director's right to be identified as the director of the film does not come into effect automatically with the creation of the copyright work in the way that copyright does. Rather it must be asserted in writing by the author before it can be enforced. Once asserted, the requirements for identification alter according to the category of work. Differences between categories that will become apparent in this section often derive from the production characteristics of the different media. For example, for reasons of scheduling time constraints, musical works included in broadcast television programmes are often not acknowledged as part of the programme's closing credits as they would be in a film. Notice that the assertion of paternity right does not cover the use of the soundtrack in a television broadcast or cable programme. Each category differs from the others in similar ways. It is important to remember that the requirement for identification depends upon the author having asserted the right in writing.

10.1.1 LITERARY AND DRAMATIC WORKS

The author of a literary or dramatic work (excluding lyrics) must be identified whenever the work is published commercially, performed in public, broadcast, included in a cable service or when copies of a film or soundtrack including the work are issued to the public.

10.1.2 MUSICAL WORKS AND LYRICS

The author of musical works and lyrics must be identified whenever the work is published commercially, a sound recording is issued to the public, a soundtrack is issued to the public or a film incorporating the soundtrack is issued to the public.

10.1.3 ARTISTIC WORKS

The author of an artistic work must be identified whenever the work is published commercially or shown in public or included in a broadcast or cable programme or included in a film which is shown in public or copies of which are issued to the public.

10.1.4 IDENTIFICATION

Any reasonable form of identification may be used in acknowledging the author, provided that both the author and the work are clearly identified and linked. Where the author has used a pseudonym, acknowledgement must be given in that form.

10.1.5 ADAPTATIONS

Adapted works, such as a condensed version of the work, a stage adaptation of a book, a translation, etc. must acknowledge the author of the original work as well as that of the adaptation.

10.2 DEROGATORY TREATMENT

While guaranteeing that an author will always receive due acknowledgement for the work is not something to concern publishers, the author's right to object to derogatory treatment may well have greater impact. Just what constitutes 'derogatory' treatment is not defined, except to say that it is more than the modifications one might expect as part of the normal editing process. It is concerned, rather, to protect the artistic integrity of the work and the author's honour and reputation. At what point treatment of the work passes from the normal changes to be expected in editing and beyond to changes that amount to a derogatory treatment is difficult to define. There is little UK case law on which to base an opinion. French law, though, is a useful guide to the approach taken by a country in which the tradition of droit moral is well established and is treated with a great deal of respect. In any event, it is no longer enough to take UK moral rights attitudes as our model. Once the production is released outside the UK, waivers obtained under UK law may no longer apply. Given the high costs of multimedia production and their reliance upon exploiting international markets, producers will depend upon the ability to market in territories such as France and others in which moral rights may be asserted.

Several cases are relevant, each of which illustrates authors' moral rights from a different perspective. By looking at these, it is possible to develop a sense of the kinds of use, particularly those made possible with multimedia developments, that may be treated as being unfair or derogatory. Much of the appeal of multimedia production depends upon its ability to manipulate, paste and colourize images and text, to extrapolate simulated action sequences from a still image. All of these capabilities have the potential to distort an author's work to such an extent that the integrity of the author, the work or both are subjected to derogatory treatment.

Example

The film director John Huston, while under contract to MGM, directed *The Asphalt Jungle*. The film was shot in black and white. The copyright in the work, as it was produced by Huston while on their staff, was MGM's. After Huston's death a colourized version of the film was developed, in which colours were artificially added by a computerized system. Huston's estate, however much they may have disliked the results, were unable to prevent the colourized version being made and subsequently released. Under the Anglo-Saxon tradition, copyright holders (in this case MGM) were free to treat their property in this way. When the film was released for television transmission in France, though, the position completely changed and the estate was able to prevent transmission of the colourized version under French moral rights legislation. Their objection was based upon the argument that the film was directed, shot, lit and designed to be screened in black and white and that hence the artistic integrity of a lauded director had been damaged by the colourization process. Three important guidelines can be derived from this example:

1. That in some circumstances colourization can be considered derogatory treatment.

---

2. That moral rights are separate from copyright, are personal to the author or their estate and can be handed down. In theory at least they can be handed down in perpetuity, so that the descendants of Leonardo da Vinci might have been able to object to Marcel Duchamp's moustachioed version of the *Mona Lisa* had it only been possible to trace them.

3. That although the colourized version of the film was free from restriction in the US, it was open to objection as soon as it was released in a territory where the moral rights of the author were recognized.

A French car company commissioned a work of modern sculpture. On completion, the company discovered that the work was not to their liking. The sculptor was paid for his work and the piece was delivered but stored in a basement rather than placed on display. The sculptor objected on the grounds that, by not displaying the work in a proper setting, the car company was subjecting it to derogatory treatment. The company was forced to display it prominently in line with the intention of the original commission. Moral rights may be infringed by including the work in a less prominent part of the production than the author expected. Might this, by extension, bring problems for the producer who commissions a work for inclusion in a multimedia production, only to find that the completed work no longer fits the production values or expectations of the product under development? Commissioning contracts should be carefully worded so as not to guarantee inclusion.

A French cable operator branded transmissions by displaying the channel logo in one corner of the television screen. A film-maker successfully objected, saying that by distracting the viewer's attention from the image on screen it amounted to derogatory treatment. The image of the logo as portrayed on screen was comparatively small in proportion to the rest of the frame and was not out of keeping with other such commonly used logos of the kind used by satellite and cable channels to brand their schedules. Yet its use was deemed sufficiently distorting to be considered derogatory treatment of the film-maker's work.

> The French fashion magazine *Vogue* ran a feature on new fashions in which Tarzan, the legendary fictitious character created in the stories of Edgar Rice Burroughs, was portrayed in a series of suggestive or provocative poses with models wearing the new season's designs. This was done without the consent of Burroughs' heirs, who sued the magazine for US$ 1 million for the unauthorized use of the Tarzan image in a way that damaged the conventional upstanding, clean-cut image of the character as it was created by Burroughs. The sexually atmospheric images, they claimed, represented a violation of the author's moral rights by distorting his original creation. Two important issues arise from this case:
>
> 1. That the portrayal of fictional characters can in certain circumstances infringe the moral rights of their creator.
> 2. That if moral rights may be infringed by the use of a fictional character, could moral rights of a performer be infringed by placing their image in unusual or unexpected surroundings?

One of the capabilities being developed in the new media is the capacity to store, manipulate and combine images taken from a variety of sources. It is possible to combine historical documentary and cinematic footage with newly shot material to produce a combination of old, reconstructed and simulated material with new, live action sequences. Films such as *Zelig*, *Forrest Gump* and *Dead Men Wear Plaid* have already made much use of these techniques and the capability of the technologies grows steadily. Multimedia production techniques allow producers to combine images of stars from the past, in their prime, with live performances by modern players, not simply by cutting together new and existing footage but by digitizing and animating single images to create entirely new interaction between the characters. Imagine, for example, Marilyn Monroe acting opposite Jack Nicholson in a new film. Could the scenes her image is manipulated to portray become a derogatory treatment of her screen persona? Looking at the use made of Tarzan in the Vogue fashion layout, the answer must be that the use of manipulated images of actors or actresses must be done with care and must take moral rights issues into account.

To date the only UK instance of a disagreement concerning moral rights reaching the courts, has concerned the popular composer and recording artist George Michael's work with his early group Wham. Several years after the demise of Wham, when Michael was strongly established as a successful solo artist, another record label released a recording called 'Bad Boys Megamix' which featured five compositions written wholly or in partnership by George Michael and originally recorded by Wham. George Michael and his publishers acted to prevent the commercial release of the 'Bad Boys Megamix' by IQ records and BMG records. The arguments were as follows:

1. Michael's publisher argued that the reproduction of the various musical works amounted to an unauthorized adaptation of the works.
2. Michael claimed that the medley, the adaptation of lyrics and the interposition of new, fill-in music amounted to derogatory treatment.
3. IQ records and BMG records denied the allegations and relied on clearance obtained from MCPS (Mechanical-Copyright Protection Society).

Michael and his publisher claimed that the licence specifically made mention of the fact that it did not cover the right to adapt the works or amount to a waiver of moral rights. Though the court found that a triable issue had been established and granted an injunction preventing the commercial release of the megamix recording, the hearing was interlocutory and so established no decision either as to what amounts to a modification or adaptation of a work or as to what constitutes derogatory treatment. Nevertheless it does go some way towards identifying the issues that might arise in similar instances of original material being licensed and subsequently being manipulated, adapted or presented in novel settings. Licensors may or may not be in a position to grant the manipulation rights that producers need and, as is the case for so many rights, it is unwise to rely upon licences without reading them carefully for authorization of the relevant rights.

10.3 EVOLVING A STRATEGY FOR MORAL RIGHTS

This chapter opened by speaking briefly of the threat raised by moral rights in the eyes of UK publishers and audio-visual producers. While the issues have to be taken seriously it is easy to overemphasize the difficulties that moral rights considerations may cause. After all, French publishers and producers, in common with those of other jurisdictions recognizing the rights of authors, are not prevented from creating products in the new media. Much of the fear arises from having to deal with a concept that is comparatively new and unknown. By evolving strategies for coping with moral rights, producers can create products to take advantage of the characteristics offered by digital formats without infringing the moral rights of the author.

The fear of loss of control is the most potent threat for many producers. While copyright can be controlled, bought or licensed, moral rights (in civil jurisdictions) can remain with the author in perpetuity, representing a production element which the producer can never fully bring under control. While moral rights may be waived within the UK, the colourization case involving *The Asphalt Jungle* shows that a UK waiver may no longer apply once the product is released in a territory, such as France, where moral rights are inalienable and unwaivable.

The evolution of a strategy to work comfortably within a moral rights framework relies upon three elements: the producer's relationship with the author, the manipulation of material in the course of production and the authorizing of manipulation by the end-user. Of the three, the development of a comfortably honest relationship with the author is the first step towards working and manipulating the material without infringement. If the author agrees to the manipulation or versioning of the work during production, then the moral rights questions are taken care of. This imposes an additional responsibility upon producers to be aware of the rights of the author when editing.

Having established a good working relationship, based upon honesty of intent, then involving the author in production decisions becomes more comfortable. This must be done with care, though, if authors making a minor contribution to the project are not to develop a heightened sense of their work's importance in relation to the whole.

Finally, producers must be careful not to act in ways which authorize others to manipulate the material. The producer can control how an author's work is treated in production. With digital systems, however, that control does not extend to the user's own manipulation of images and text. There is little a producer can do to prevent a user from creating their own version of material supplied on disk. What can be done is to inform the user of the restrictions of copyright and moral rights applying to the product and to avoid licensing or authorizing the user to infringe those rights. Producers, particularly of educational products where demonstrating particular techniques may involve manipulation of the work, must be extremely careful not to direct students to act in ways which infringe.

Negotiation tips and hints

11

You will by now have gathered that successful rights clearance relies on being able to negotiate satisfactory deals. Successful negotiation could be defined as getting as good an outcome as possible on behalf of the interests you represent and reaching an outcome that will last and may set a precedent for the future. It is about getting somewhere without a breakdown in communication. But how do you negotiate successfully?

11.1 SUCCESSFUL NEGOTIATION

Everyone will probably have been a negotiator at some time in their life. If you have bought a house or a car the chances are that you negotiated for it; you may have to carry out negotiations with family members all the time about what to watch on television or where to go on holiday. If you are employed you may have to negotiate your salary or your job description, but have you ever thought about the steps in successful negotiating and how to best achieve the desired outcome?

As every Boy Scout will tell you the first rule to follow to achieve a successful negotiation is: be prepared. You must know what you want and why you want it, when you want it, how much you need it, what your options are if you cannot get it. Remember, therefore: fail to prepare, prepare to fail. Once you start to negotiate, listen to what the person you are negotiating with wants – what their concerns are. Also ensure that you are understood. Does the person you are negotiating with understand what you want? Negotiating is all about flexibility.

Good negotiation

1. *Negotiate with the right person/company.*
2. *Know the time scale you have to reach agreement.*

3. *If making an offer, be realistic with your first offer.*
4. *Do not increase/decrease too much too soon.*
5. *Separate the person from the problem (it is not who is right but what is right).*
6. *Want what you are negotiating for (without being over eager) and be confident.*
7. *If offering, understand the basis of the fee you offer.*
8. *Believe what you offer is right. (If you do not, why are you offering it?)*
9. *Do not fill silence (do not waffle).*
10. *Always give yourself time to think.*
11. *Not all negotiations will result in a deal.*
12. *Do not attack or defend.*
13. *Once an agreement is made, make sure that both sides fulfil their promise.*
14. *Beware of 'favoured nations' settlements (i.e. agreeing to something with one party because they are to be treated better than other parties you deal with).*

11.2 OFFERS

Negotiation for rights is normally about one party wishing to make use of something over which another party exercises control. Therefore the negotiations usually start with an offer of money or a request for rights.

11.2.1 MAKING OFFERS

When making an offer allow room for manoeuvre; do not lock yourself to the first offer you make. When you make your offer do not offer the maximum available straight away unless you are offering a standard fee or something that you cannot improve on and you are prepared to not reach agreement.

It is important to encourage trust – you are not there to rip people off. It is vital to encourage good working relationships when negotiating. Give the people you negotiate with confidence that you are the one to make decisions. Never say, 'I will have to check if I can offer more.' Say instead, 'I will have to think about the increase and the possible effects it will cause; I will get back to you.' If the rate is not negotiable do not get intimidated, feel comfortable with the offer you make and be clear that it is the right amount. Feel free to justify the amount you offer, explain your circumstances and the reasons for the amount offered, but always be comfortable with the amount.

Sometimes when making an offer you will have to pay more than you want to. This need not be a terrible outcome. Remember that the aim of any negotiation is to reach an agreement that is acceptable to both or all parties;

it is not about coercion. As long as the sum agreed is within your acceptable limits you cannot say that the negotiation has been a failure.

If your offer is refused, what do you do then? You need to plan for a refusal, and know what you are going to say. You can ask questions: 'Why do you think the amount you want is fair?' or, 'Why do you think my proposal will present you with difficulties?' Allow the other person to 'blow off steam' without taking it personally. Do not make any threats to the other person. If they are unreasonable or unpleasant try to remain calm and professional and try to gain some breathing space.

It is quite common for someone receiving an offer simply to refuse or to ask for more. Never accept 'I want more money' without getting the other person to give their reasons. Do not reveal another contributor's fee or deal: would you like strangers to know your salary? If you are asked what you are paying others, say instead: 'The other fees are in the same area,' or, 'This is what I am offering to all contributors.' If you cannot improve your offer, know why and be prepared to explain the reasons for or basis of what you are offering to begin with. Be prepared to admit to the precedents you have agreed (without breaching confidentiality) and the principles that you used to work out the fee.

Be fair to your own interests and to theirs, but do not provide the other person with weapons that they may turn on you. This can be a difficult road to travel. You must not mislead the other party – they must understand the terms of the contract you are making – but think about the words you use to describe the offer. You need to paint your own case in its best light; do not undersell yourself. Everyone knows that an estate agent's particulars make the best of the property they are trying to sell, and they accept that. You will be expected to do the same about the offer you are making. If you are too eager to explain the negative aspects of the offer, you will only encourage the other person to think the final product is a dud. However, do not run the risk of having your contributor reneging on the deal by lying about the product or engagement.

11.2.2 RECEIVING OFFERS

Some people are instantly suspicious on receiving an offer of money; others cannot wait to agree. It is all about self-confidence. You feel either that you are worth the earth or that you will never be offered another bean so you had better accept anything you are offered, no matter how derisory. This may be fine if you do not have to earn your living in this way and the negotiation is a one-off, never to be repeated, but can you ever be sure that this is the case?

If possible, try to distance yourself from the work or material being discussed. If you cannot do this, consider engaging an agent to act on your behalf. When an offer is made, think about it. The best agents always just listen to any offer made, and unless it is entirely standard they say nothing and ask for some thinking time. Try to do the same – do not allow the offerer to pressurize you into a decision. Then you have time to consider the offer. Is it reasonable or do you require more? If you do want more, what are your reasons? If the offerer will not offer more, are you prepared to refuse? Do some research into the field if this is new to you. Once you feel comfortable with the work in question and the points you wish to make, continue with the negotiation.

The offerer may wish to set a time limit for thinking. This may be entirely fair, as decisions do need to be made, but make sure you are comfortable with the time allowed. Try not to get angry or abusive with the person making the offer. If they are rude to you, do not react in a like manner. You can let them know the way you feel without being rude.

When you do speak again to the person making the offer, remember the parameters you have set yourself. If the final agreement is within those parameters you have every reason to feel content with yourself.

11.3 TYPES AND STYLES OF NEGOTIATION

11.3.1 THREE TYPES OF NEGOTIATION

There are three types of negotiation commonly used in rights clearance: telephone, letter and face-to-face. The most commonly used are telephone and letter, or a combination of the two. The usual style expected by the people you will be negotiating with depends on the specific business they are in. Offers made for people to perform are normally made by phone, followed sometimes by letter. Music clearance is negotiated both over the phone and by letter. Publishers usually like to work by letter. Film companies would expect to negotiate by phone. Face-to-face negotiations would be more usual for very large deals, and for group negotiation.

Each type of negotiation has its own pros and cons (Table 11.1).

11.3.2 STYLES OF NEGOTIATION

It is said that there are four P's to negotiation: Purpose, Plan, Pace and Personality. What is the **purpose** of the negotiation? Always be clear before you begin to negotiate what exactly you are aiming for. **Plan** your strategy, know as much as possible about what you are negotiating for. If you are requesting permission to use material or trying to engage someone to work for you, be clear about what you will do with the material or the result of the work. When negotiating for rights, as has been discussed in the previous chapters, you need to be careful to know what use you will make of material. However, even if you know what use you require, you may still need to prepare for the chance that your use will be denied. Prepare your list of

Table 11.1 Types of negotiation

Type	Pros	Cons
Telephone		
	Fast response	No written record
	You decide when to ring	Little time for thought
	You have notes to refer to	You may be calling at an awkward time
	Your body language is not visible	Their body language is not visible
	More interest at work	You have to follow it up with writing
	Early warning of potential difficulties	Clarity (one side thinking 50 was agreed, the other side 15)
	Tone of voice/accent	Tone of voice/accent
	Pause	Pause
	Personality/rapport	Personality/rapport
	In control	Out of control
Letter/fax		
	Written record	They may have moved/on holiday
	Time to think	Not addressed to relevant person/no one takes action
		No opportunity for intuition
Face to face		
	Body language is visible	Body language is visible
	More chance of a resolution	Notes not easily used

options, should your first request be refused. Never say 'no' unless it really is 'no' and you can do without the material. Always consider what the other options are first.

Preparation

1. *Ask colleagues what is a realistic offer.*
2. *Find out the use to which the material will be put (actual and potential).*

3. *Find out what the person/company is like to negotiate with by asking colleagues.*
4. *Decide if you need to clear more now to save you a job later on.*
5. *Look at similar deals that have been agreed.*
6. *Ask unions/trade associations if they have any minimum rates for what you require.*
7. *Check with similar companies/people what their rate would be for what you require.*
8. *Confirm what you are negotiating for with the people that require it.*
9. *If you are being asked for something that goes against current thinking/practice, check first.*
10. *As a last resort ask the person/company that you are negotiating with if they have any view as to what the job or material is worth.*

Pace, or timing, is the next of the four P's. Give yourself time to negotiate. The amount of time it takes to negotiate rights clearances can be considerable and is probably the most underestimated fact in many a project. If you are a producer of material you could consider that you are operating at the mercy of the rights holders. The more time you give yourself to achieve your aims, the easier the process will be. Do not put yourself into the position of having to carry out too many negotiations at the eleventh hour. People who know you are desperate will often feel more than happy to exploit that.

You must, however, engender some feeling of urgency in those with whom you negotiate. You do not want everything to drag on for weeks. You must encourage people to make decisions and sign contracts and letters. This feeling that the matter is important and needs to be attended to, but is not a matter where the rights holder has the other party over a barrel will depend on the negotiator's personality.

The **personality** of the negotiator is a vital element of the whole process. You need to understand your personality and to realize in what areas you are not persuasive enough to be a successful negotiator. Once you understand your own strengths and weaknesses you can act upon them, and adapt your own style to enable a satisfactory end result.

Acting and reacting

1. *Be yourself but remember you are doing a job and therefore do not take it personally.*
2. *Do not mirror the style of the people with whom you negotiate.*
3. *Aim in a business field to achieve long-term solutions without jeopardizing a potential long-term relationship.*
4. *Aim to achieve a positive relationship rather than a personal relationship.*

5. *If the person you are speaking to becomes personally abusive remind them that this is a business discussion, repeat your offer suggesting they think about it and say you will contact them again on a given date.*

Many people are familiar with modern views on assertive behaviour. It is often promoted as being the ideal way to conduct life in a crowded world. It would also appear to be the ideal way in which to carry out negotiations but you cannot always work in ideal circumstances. Table 11.2 gives some of the characteristics of negotiating in the three given styles: aggressive, assertive and passive. If you aim to negotiate deals which will last and provide a basis for future agreements, then the assertive style would appear to be the preferred style. However, if you are able to analyse your own style and adapt it, you will be in a very advantageous position as you can choose which style to adopt in any given situation.

Table 11.2   Styles of negotiation

Aggressive	Assertive	Passive
Competitive	Co-operative	Giving in
Rigid	Flexible	Door mat
Personal	Negotiating points	No discussion
Win/lose and lose/lose	Win/win	Lose/lose and lose/win
Victor/victim		Victim/loser
Short-term or no solution	Long-term solution	Short-term or no solution
No basis for a future deal	Basis for future deal	Basis for being ripped off next time

11.4 SOME TIPS ON THINGS TO SAY

When you make an offer and it is rejected, there are some fairly common reasons given for refusing the fee and asking for more money. You need to be aware of these and also of how to answer them. Remember that the aim is to achieve a satisfactory outcome where both parties are content. You might have to reassure the other party that you are trying to be fair, that you have given careful thought to the offer and that you wish to reach an amicable agreement.

Common rejections of a first offer include:

- You are going to make a lot of money out of this so why shouldn't I?
- I hear that X got ...
- What did X get for this?
- Is this the best you can offer? (Be careful not to just say, 'Yes.' Instead, say: 'Given all the facts, yes,' or, 'It is a fair fee for the rights I wish to buy.')
- I got twice as much last week!
- We charge/my rate is ...
- I accepted your offer last time and then found out you had offered more to ...
- I was told I was going to get ...
- I am irreplaceable, you must pay me ...
- I have got a wife and two children to support.
- I give my daughter more in pocket money.
- I want the top fee.
- Remember my (the agent's) 20%.

In response, here are some useful replies:

- It is in line with other fees.
- It is comparable to contributors/contributions of similar status.
- It is a fair fee.
- This is not a precedent.
- This is a first time fee, I will review the offer next time.
- It may not appear much but it is in line with the budget.
- This is for an educational market, not mass market.
- I have spoken with colleagues and they agree ...
- Perhaps there is another way that we can work this out.
- If this offer is not accepted we will have to think seriously about re-casting/deleting the material.
- I realize you will be disappointed but I am not able to increase my offer.
- I do not feel this negotiation is going forward. Can I just reiterate my offer?
- What is being asked for is unreasonable. (Not: 'You are being unreasonable.')
- If you can agree to this then you will gain by ...

Summing up

When summing up, bear the following points in mind:

- *Do not end with: 'If this is OK with you?'*
  Say: 'I think this is a fair fee', rather than: 'Do you agree this is a fair fee?'
- *Summarize at the end of each communication and if face-to-face at regular intervals to reinforce the offer (repetition has a habit of becoming fact).*

You may well be asked to explain how you have decided upon a fee. Unless it is an agreed union rate or standard fee, be general in your explanation. Say something like: 'It is based on similar fees that we have paid for similar work.' Do not reveal other fees; keep the discussion general. If the offer is an agreed union or associated body rate, suggest that the person being offered the fee should take it up with the union or association but that in the meantime they should accept your offer. You will obviously have to be certain that the rate is acceptable to the union or association.

Tips on the phone

Many negotiations are carried out by phone. You may feel unsure of yourself on the phone, so try to make life easy for yourself.

1. *Stand up (it gives you more confidence).*
2. *Be clear.*
3. *Do not feel pressurized into agreeing everything in one call.*
4. *Be businesslike until you feel confident to adapt to the caller's style.*
5. *Do not fill gaps.*
6. *Do not increase the offer or reduce the charge during the first phone call.*
7. *Confirm what has been agreed.*
8. *If they hang up: call them back after 15 minutes, suggest you have been cut off and reiterate your offer (use your discretion in doing this).*
9. *End positively: 'I will write confirming our deal,' or: 'I will expect your reply in ... days.'*
10. *Talk to people who sound unsure, giving them confidence that you know what you are talking about and giving them less time to think.*
11. *Listen to professional negotiators with whom you want to negotiate, giving yourself time to think up answers and not giving you the chance to put your foot in it.*

11.5 DIFFICULT NEGOTIATIONS

Match an impossible demand with another impossible demand to force an opening for negotiation. For example, if the demand is: 'I want £2500 for you to use this photograph,' respond by saying: 'If we were to pay that amount we would want exclusive use in all media throughout the world in perpetuity.' If the response comes back, 'I will not give those rights!', you have an opening to say, 'In that case what do you want for all rights for 5 years?' Try to separate the person from the problem and maintain a professional distance. If the person you are dealing with locks themselves into a stand early on, ask them what their worries are and try to get them to explain their concerns; you might then be able to open up the discussion.

If the other party persists with their stand you might feel that you will have to give way. Before doing so, be sure that you have no alternative. Think about the worst deal that is acceptable rather than your normal bottom line and try to achieve this. If you end up feeling that you are having to agree to an unreasonable resolution, stop and think. Must you choose this step? You could always decide to not make an agreement and abort the negotiation. Once you decide that you will give in on an important point, you can try to salvage something from the encounter. Insist that this agreement will not be taken as a precedent. Could you perhaps sweeten this pill in a way that will not have an effect on further deals? Remember that it is possible to improve an offer for one side without it necessarily being worse for the other. If you are presented with an unreasonable offer or demand do not discuss it but present your own reasonable offer or demand. If you do end up feeling that the deal made is a poor one for you or your company, you will just have to chalk it up to experience.

Production paperwork

12

Throughout this book you have been told how to clear third party material, but as important as getting the clearance is being able to keep track of this clearance. When offers or requests are made it is vital to be able to know what stage of clearance any piece of material has reached. It is important to keep up the momentum of clearance, and to chase up responses in order to ensure clearance is made in time for the project to be produced.

It may be necessary to set up systems for the maintenance of these clearance records and a chase-up system. These records have a tendency to run away with themselves. If you have any quantity of third party material you may find it takes all your time to track it and clear it. It will pay you to be organized in the long run.

12.1 PROGRAMME DOCUMENTATION

Having cleared all the material used in your project, you will probably heave a sigh of relief and hope never to have to look into any of it again! However, the truth of the matter is that you need to keep thorough records of what you have used and what permissions you have been granted. It is of no use at all to clear the material used in your project if there is not some form of written proof that you have done so.

The first step in your record keeping is to prepare a comprehensive report of the content of the programme or project.

If you are producing text the tracing of third party materials within the finished book is not difficult, but if you are producing a television programme it is not so easy to look for and find every piece of material. When producing other electronic or interactive materials (a CD-ROM, for example) keeping track of third party material becomes ever more difficult.

Television and radio producers have dealt with this problem by the use of 'Programme as Complete' (PasC) or 'Programme as Broadcast' (PasB) forms. These log every component of a finished programme, listing not only the material used but also the contract terms under which it was used. The forms show details of when a programme was first broadcast, the tape number on which it is stored and other matters useful for archiving purposes. The information stored on these forms regarding rights clearance enables an experienced person to judge quickly the likely implications of any use made of the programme.

As Figure 12.1 shows, the PasC form is broken into sections which reflect the breakdown of chapters in this book: people, pictures, graphics, film footage, written material and music. The reason for these traditional divisions is that each area has evolved its own standards and standard contracts, and the practices of rights clearance in one area differ from those in another. However, as has been demonstrated in earlier chapters, the results of the rights clearance process should give the producers or owners of the final product the right to use the material as they desire.

It is essential to be able to look at a programme or product as a sum of its component parts in order to clarify what material has been used and what rights need to be cleared. If a producer wishes to use an actor performing a scripted piece of material involving the use of a piece of artwork and some recorded music, the simplest way to ensure that each piece of work is properly contracted is to break the piece down into its parts. Thus you see that:

1. You need to contract an actor.
2. You need to clear the written material.
3. You need to clear the artwork.
4. You need to clear the music.

The written record of these actions then fits neatly into the division of different materials on the PasC or PasB form.

For the producer of a non-linear product such as a CD-ROM, the production of a PasC (perhaps renamed for the computer age) is even more critical. Material of the sort used by television and video producers can still be listed as shown on the PasC, but it is likely to be more difficult to trace the material on a CD-ROM than on a television or video programme. Any hypertext surrounding the material should also be listed.

A CD-ROM will also contain other material which has been cleared for use on the CD-ROM, most notably software. It is essential that this is also recorded on the PasC. It is not easy to 'see' the software when using the product – there might be an acknowledgement of it as a condition of its use but the where and how of its use will probably be invisible. This is why a proper written record is essential. It would be sensible to draw up a form of PasC as a list of material used by tracing the various routes through the screen displays of the CD-ROM. It is extremely common today for records to be stored electronically, and there is no problem at all about this when

PROGRAMME AS COMPLETED FORM (PAGE 1 OF 4)

PROGRAMME TITLE:

SUB TITLE:

EPISODE NUMBER:

FORMAT:	VT1" C.	VT2" QUAD	FILM	FILM	OTHER
(PLEASE	BETA SP	D3 D5	16mm	35mm	(SPECIFY)
ENCIRCLE)	STEREO	MONO	SEPMAG	COMMAG OPT.	

RUNNING TIME:

NAME OF PRODUCTION COMPANY:

NAME OF PRODUCER/DIRECTOR: TEL:

ADDRESS: HOME TEL:

OTHER USEFUL CONTACTS: NAME: TEL:

PROGRAMME SYNOPSIS (ABOUT 120 WORDS)

CAST LIST:

SIGNATURE.. DATE..................................

PROGRAMME AS COMPLETED FORM   (PAGE 2 OF 4)

COPYRIGHT MATERIAL

SET OUT IN RESPECT OF ALL COPYRIGHT MATERIAL (i.e. STILLS OR FILM/VT FOOTAGE etc.) INCORPORATED IN THE PROGRAMME

PROGRAMME TITLE:

DESCRIPTION	SOURCE OF MATERIAL	FEE	RIGHTS OBTAINED e.g. UK TV WORLD NON-THEATRIC (Length of Licence Period) etc.	COST FOR FURTHER RIGHTS
a) STILLS				
b) ARCHIVE FOOTAGE				
c) SCRIPT (ORIGINAL AND ADAPTATION)/ QUOTATIONS etc.				

PROGRAMME AS COMPLETED FORM

RIGHTS

PLEASE COMPLETE THE RELEVANT SECTION(S) BELOW IN RESPECT OF ALL MUSIC INCORPORATED IN THE PROGRAMME

PROGRAMME TITLE:

DESCRIPTION	SOURCE OF MATERIAL/ RECORD LABEL NO. AND NAME OF COMPOSER/ ARRANGER	FEE	RIGHTS OBTAINED e.g. UK TV WORLD NON-THEATRIC (Length of Licence Period) etc.	COST FOR FURTHER RIGHTS
a) LIBRARY MUSIC/ DISCS				
b) COMMERCIAL MUSIC/ RECORDS				
c) COMMISS- IONED MUSIC				

* PLEASE OBTAIN QUOTE/ESTIMATE FOR (1) WORLD TV (INCLUDING PAY/CABLE), (2) WORLD NON-THEATRIC, (3) WORLD VIDEO. IF POSSIBLE, THIS SHOULD BE DONE ON A TERRITORY BY TERRITORY BASIS. PLEASE STATE IF ANY RESTRICTIONS ON RIGHTS AVAILABLE.

PROGRAMME AS COMPLETED FORM

CONTRIBUTORS

PLEASE LIST BELOW THE NAME AND ADDRESS OF EACH CONTRIBUTOR OR THEIR AGENT, STATING IN EACH CASE:

a) THE UNION AGREEMENT (i.e. PACT etc.)
b) FEE PLUS RIGHTS ACQUIRED
c) WHERE THERE ARE ANY SPECIAL CONDITIONS OR RESTRICTIONS IN CONTRACTS WITH EQUITY OR OTHER UNION MEMBERS PLEASE INDICATE

ALWAYS ATTACH COPIES OF ALL CONTRACTS.

CHARACTER	NAME OF ARTIST ADDRESS	NAME OF AGENT ADDRESS	UNION AGREEMENT OR RIGHTS ACQUIRED	FEE	REPEAT RESIDUALS	N.I. NO.	V.A.T. NO.

talking about a PasC or the summary of the product content, however the copies of letters and contracts relating to rights clearances need to be stored as paper copies with real signatures.

Appendix A gives sample letters and contracts that can be adapted for use in project production. It is a good idea to produce a series of shell letters and contracts for use in your project and to keep these as templates on computer. Do, however, be aware that you might need to adapt your standard contracts and letters as the occasion demands and to write one-off documents as the need arises.

Appendix A Examples of letters and contracts

A.1 *Example of a letter seeking permission for use of material in a book*

Rights and Permissions
The Publisher
The Street
The Town
The County

Ref

Dear Sir/Madam

In xxxx the X Press is/I am to publish a book entitled xxxxxxxx. Within the text I/we would like to use the following material in English (and in Braille and sound recording for the blind).

Author: (Name)
Publication: (Book Title)
Chapter: (Chapter No and Title)
Page No(s):   (Pages)
No of Words: (Number)

I/We wish to distribute the publication in the world market.

The proposed print run will be approximately xxxxx copies.

I/We enclose a photocopy of the material to be used.

I/We hope that you will be able to grant me/us permission to use this material for which full acknowledgement will be made. If you do not control the rights to the material mentioned above, I/we would be most grateful for the name and address of the copyright holder concerned.

I/We appreciate your co-operation in making this material available and would ask you to kindly return this complete document duly signed.

Yours faithfully

Ref:

Permission is hereby granted for the use of the above mentioned material.

Signed _____ Title _____

Company/Publisher* _____ Date _____
* Please delete as appropriate

A.2   *Example of a letter seeking permission for use of material on a CD-ROM*

Rights and Permissions
The Publisher
The Street
The Town
The County

Our Ref:

Dear Sir/Madam

I/We are working on the production of a CD-ROM entitled xxxxxxxxxxx for use in xxxxxxxxxx. It will be used by xxxxxxxxx, and distributed by xxxxxxxxxx. I/We wish to include on the CD-ROM the following material for which I/we believe you hold the copyright:

Author: (Name)
Publication: (Book Title)
Chapter: (Chapter No and Title)
Page No(s):   (Pages)
No of Words: (Number)

I/We hope that you will be able to grant us permission to use this material for which full acknowledgement will be made. If you do not control the rights to the material mentioned above, I/we would be most grateful for the name and address of the copyright holder concerned.

Similarly, if you require the author's approval we would be most grateful for full details.

We appreciate your co-operation in making this material available and would ask you to kindly return this complete document duly signed.

Yours

Ref:

Permission is hereby granted for the use of the above mentioned material.

Signed _____ Title _____

Company/Publisher* _____ Date _____

* Please delete as appropriate

A.3 *Royalties: example of a letter extending rights to sell programmes following an agreement with Equity*

Rights Department
The Open University
Walton Hall
Milton Keynes
MK7 6AA
United Kingdom

25 October 1994

Telephone (01908) 274066
Direct Line (01908) 65
Telex 825061
Fax (01908) 654322

Joe Bloggs
2 Street Road
London
SW1 4XX

Production: **"Sergeant Musgrave's Dance"**
Contract Date: **22 May 1990**

I am writing in connection with the above contract to confirm that the xxx Production Company and the British Actors Equity Association have reached an agreement over the distribution of royalties on sales of the above production whereby each contributor receives a royalty based on the relationship of his or her initial fee to the total initial fees paid to contributors and copyright holders for the production. The total royalty to be distributed in this way amounts to ten per cent (10%) of the retail price of the cassette, less VAT.

The royalty payable to you per sale is **3p**. It is possible that discounting of the cassette may take place, but the royalty shown **is guaranteed on all sales**. Obviously, if it is necessary for us to increase prices, this too will be reflected in the amount of royalty due.

We propose to send you payment together with a statement of royalty earnings annually.

Would you kindly signify acceptance of royalties on the basis described above by signing and returning one copy of this letter to me as soon as possible.

Yours sincerely

(Name)

I accept payment of the royalty shown above:

Signed:- .... **Date:-**...

A.4 *Model release form*

Name of Photographer/Publisher
Address

Product in which Photograph(s) will be used

In consideration of the fee of £xx.xx and any other sums that may become due to me, I permit the Photographer/Publisher and its licensees or assigns to use the photograph(s) and/or drawings therefrom and any other reproductions or adaptations thereof either complete or in part, alone or in conjunction with any wording and/or drawings for all advertising and/or publicity and/or editorial purposes in connection with the above product or service in the United Kingdom and/or any other country overseas.

Unless otherwise agreed, the photograph(s) and any drawings or adaptations thereof shall be deemed to represent an imaginary person.

I understand that I do not own the copyright in the photograph(s).

I am over 16 years of age.

Name...
Address

Signed... Date...

A.5   *Example of an agreement relating to the acquisition of written material for inclusion in a television or radio programme*

SCHEDULE

The Contributor: ....
of
....
....
....
....

The Programme: ....

The Material: ....

The Agreed Fee: ....

This agreement is made between the CONTRIBUTOR specified above as the CONTRIBUTOR of the one part ("the CONTRIBUTOR") and .... ("the CONTRACTOR") of the other part.

WHEREAS:
the CONTRACTOR wishes to use the work with the title(s) specified above and the CONTRIBUTOR has agreed upon the terms and conditions set out in this agreement that such work may be used in connection with the programme specified in the schedule above and to grant to the CONTRACTOR certain rights as hereinafter set out

NOW IT IS HEREBY AGREED AS FOLLOWS:

I DEFINITIONS

In this agreement

1. **"Additional Rights"** means the rights set out in Clause IV below.

2. **"Basic Rights"** means the rights set out in Clause III below.

3. **"Basic Rights Period"** means the period of 10 years from the date of first transmission by the CONTRACTOR of the Work.

4. **"Programme"** means the radio or television programmes, brief details of which are set out in the schedule above.

5. **"Recording"** means any recording of a television or radio programme made by any means now or hereafter devised.

6. **"Work"** means the material known by the title(s) specified in the schedule above.

II GRANT

1. **IN CONSIDERATION** of the CONTRACTOR's undertaking to pay to the CONTRIBUTOR or his/her agent the Initial Fee specified above and any additional fees specified in this agreement

(a) The CONTRIBUTOR hereby authorises the CONTRACTOR to use the Work in the Programme and for such other purposes set out in this Agreement as the CONTRACTOR may require; and

(b) the CONTRIBUTOR hereby grants to the CONTRACTOR the Basic Rights and the Additional Rights.

2. Payment of the Initial Fee shall be as soon as practicable after recording of the programme by the CONTRACTOR.

3. The grant of the Basic Rights and the Additional Rights shall not impose any obligation on the CONTRACTOR to exercise such rights.

III BASIC RIGHTS

The Basic Rights are unless otherwise stated exercisable during the Basic Rights Period (and any extension thereof under Clause IV 1). The Basic Rights are:

1. the right to make Recordings including the Work and to give up to 10 television broadcasts (or 18 if so specified) thereof simultaneously or non-simultaneously by any method or technique including the use of transmitters in the UK.

2. the right to permit the Work to be recorded "off the air" by institutions of further or higher education and schools for use solely in their own courses for a period of 5 years from the date when such "off the air" recordings are made.

3. the right to reproduce the Work in whole or in part in printed form and, if considered necessary by the CONTRACTOR, in edited form for issue to students and staff of the CONTRACTOR.

4. the right to use and permit the use of the Work and Recordings including the Work for making, broadcasting and exploiting programmes incorporating the Work which contain descriptions of a performance of the Work on a separate audio channel (or by any other means whether now known or hereafter invented) in the form of an audio description of the visual elements of the programmes incorporating the Work for the purpose of assisting those who are visually impaired.

5. the right at any time to use the Work or Recordings including the Work for:

    (a) the private purposes of the CONTRACTOR including staff training;

    (b) broadcasting brief excerpts in programmes of an historic or reminiscent nature or for trailer purposes;

    (c) deposit, if such Recording is considered of permanent interest, with the National Sound Archive and the National Film Archive (being part of the British Film Institute) and with similar archive holding bodies for presentation purposes and for private study on the premises by bona fide students; and

    (d) purposes of educational research and demonstration throughout the world, and at international education festivals and competitions.

IV ADDITIONAL RIGHTS

The Additional Rights are, unless otherwise stated, exercisable during the Basic Rights Period and any extension thereof under Clause IV 1. The Additional Rights are:

1. the right by notice to the CONTRIBUTOR to extend the Basic Rights Period and the right to give repeat television broadcasts of Recordings including the Work or substantial extracts therefrom simultaneously or non-simultaneously by any method or technique including the use of transmitters in the UK subject to payment of an additional 25% of the Initial Fee or pro rata in proportion to the amount of the extract used as to the whole of the Work for every 2 (two) additional broadcasts, payable on broadcast of the first of each such additional 2 (two) broadcasts.

2. the right to supply Recordings including the Work for showing in English or translated or dubbed into a foreign language throughout the World in any television medium howsoever delivered whether now known or thereafter devised including pay or otherwise including (but without limitation) by means of standard television and non-standard television including (but without limitation) any form of cable or satellite without restriction as to the number of showings or the length of any licence period granted to a purchaser subject to payment of

    ....

V WARRANTIES/CONDITIONS/GENERAL

1. The CONTRIBUTOR shall disclose to the CONTRACTOR such parts of the Work as are not his or her original work and shall further disclose if he or she is the assignee of copyright in such parts and whether in any such assignment the rights in Section 77 of the Copyright, Designs and Patents Act 1988 have been asserted by the assignor. Save as so disclosed the CONTRIBUTOR warrants that:

    (a) he or she is entitled to grant to the CONTRACTOR all rights granted pursuant to this Agreement;

    (b) the grant of rights to the CONTRACTOR contained herein does not conflict with rights granted to or belonging to any other party.

2. The CONTRIBUTOR hereby indemnifies and keeps the CONTRACTOR indemnified against any costs, damages and legal expenses incurred by or given against the CONTRACTOR by reason of breach of warranty by the CONTRIBUTOR.

3. For the avoidance of doubt nothing in this agreement shall prevent the CONTRACTOR from making any use of the Work for which the consent of the CONTRIBUTOR is not required by law and no payment shall be due in respect of any such use.

4. Any notice required to be given to the CONTRIBUTOR shall be given in writing to the CONTRIBUTOR at the address shown in the schedule above.

5. This Agreement shall be governed by English Law and the parties hereto agree to submit to the jurisdiction of the English Courts.

7. The CONTRACTOR and the CONTRIBUTOR agree that, notwithstanding anything to the contrary (whether oral or written) contained in any other documentation relating to the supply, reproduction or payment for the Work including (without limitation) the CONTRIBUTOR's delivery notes or invoices, this Agreement contains the entire understanding of the parties in relation to the reproduction of the Work itself including the warranties and indemnities relating to the use of the Work the fees payable for reproduction, payment obligations, credits and the manner in which the Work will be used.

A.6   *Example of terms and conditions for an all-rights contract for a contribution to a television or radio programme*

1. In consideration of the fee specified in the attached offer of engagement ("the fee") the Contributor agrees with the Producer ("the Producer") to make the contribution for use in or in connection with broadcast programmes and for such other purposes mentioned in this Agreement as the Producer may require.

2. If the Contributor is required to produce a script for the contribution, then such script shall be delivered to the PRODUCER not later than the date shown in the attached offer of engagement or such later date as may be agreed by the PRODUCER. In the event of the script not being delivered by the due date, it shall be open to the PRODUCER by notice to the Contributor to cancel this engagement forthwith and any liability on the part of the PRODUCER to make further payments under this Agreement shall thereupon cease. The contribution shall conform to the script as finally accepted by the PRODUCER. The Contributor further agrees, if required, to provide short descriptive notes on the contribution for possible inclusion in the published programmes of the PRODUCER and/or any other material (including suggestions and book lists) to be used in the issue of any publication relating to the contribution. If the contribution contains a scripted element for use of which a foreign or domestic collecting society grants or administers a licence, the contributor should report it to such society so that any payment due to the Contributor may be made. The contributor shall not be entitled to payment for such use from the PRODUCER nor shall they lay claim to any monies payable by the society in respect thereof. In particular the Contributor shall not be entitled to payment from the PRODUCER where under such licence the script(s) as incorporated in the PRODUCER's programme(s) are included in a cable programme service or are otherwise transmitted outside the United Kingdom in accordance with Clause 9 hereof.

3. The Contributor shall at reasonable time before the contribution is first recorded hereunder disclose to the PRODUCER such parts as are not his original work and shall further disclose if he is the assignee of copyright in such work and in which assignment the rights in Section 77 of the Copyright, Designs and Patents Act 1988 have been asserted by the assignor. The Contributor warrants that to the best of his knowledge and belief the contribution is not calculated to bring the PRODUCER into disrepute or an infringement of copyright or defamatory (provided that he shall not be liable in respect of any defamatory matter which was included without negligence or malice on his part). The Contributor hereby waives all his moral rights or so called droit moral as the author of the contribution including, but without limitation, any rights under Sections 77 and 80 of the Copyright, Designs and Patents Act 1988.

4. The contribution (including any exhibit(s) provided by the Contributor) shall not contain any advertisement or any matter of an advertising character.

5. The Contributor shall not prior to the first broadcast of the contribution by the PRODUCER make or authorise the making of any other contribution having a substantially similar content for any other broadcasting organisation without the prior consent in writing of the PRODUCER.

6. The Contributor agrees to attend such rehearsals as shall be considered necessary by the PRODUCER and such recording and/or broadcast sessions as shall be reasonably required by the PRODUCER. The details shown in the attached offer of engagement with regard to the dates, times and places of rehearsals, recordings and broadcasts are for guidance only and may be changed by the PRODUCER as circumstances may reasonably require.

7. The Contributor agrees to be made up (if required) by a person appointed by the PRODUCER and to wear such article(s) of costume in place of those provided by the Contributor as may be required by the PRODUCER to ensure satisfactory reception of the Contributor's picture on the receiving screen.

8. (a) The "contribution" means the part taken in accordance with this Agreement by the Contributor in the television programme(s) described in the attached offer of engagement and, where applicable, includes the script prepared by the Contributor for use in or in connection with such programme(s) and any exhibit(s) or other material provided by the Contributor.

   (b) A "recording" means the aggregate of sounds and/or visual images embodied in material of any description and capable of being reproduced by means of a mechanical contrivance.

9. Without further payment the PRODUCER shall be entitled (except as provided in Clause 10) to ALL RIGHTS in the contribution (including any recording(s) or translations(s) thereof) EVERYWHERE AND FOR ALL PURPOSES. Such rights shall include but shall not be limited to:

   (a) all Television and Radio broadcasting (including broadcasting and other forms of transmission by wire and/or cable and/or satellites) rights;

   (b) the right to show or authorise the showing of the contribution(s) to paying and non-paying audiences (including the right to sell or hire for such purposes);

   (c) The right to incorporate the contribution in a videogram(s) (which shall mean videocassettes, videodiscs and any other device for reproducing visual images and sound which may be played back by the use of a playback device) and the right to sell or hire or authorise the sale or hire of such videogram(s) to the public for home use;

   (d) the right to show or authorise the showing of the contribution on pay television pay cable television basic cable television and by means of all other forms of television distribution whether now existing or developed in the future (including by satellites);

   (e) the right to adapt and modify and make other use of any material and scripts supplied by you for promotional and/or demonstration purposes;

   (f) the right to edit or abridge the contribution and the rights granted to the PRODUCER under this contract shall apply to the whole or any excerpt(s) from the contribution;

   (g) the right to broadcast as required for trailer purposes:
       (i) extracts (live and recorded) from the contribution or any rehearsal(s) thereof;
       (ii) material (live or recorded) specially contributed by you for trailer programmes and not requiring a separate attendance;

   (h) the right to permit the contribution to be recorded "off the air" by ERA licensees;

   (i) the right to reproduce the contribution in whole or in part in printed form and if necessary in edited form for issue to students and staff of the PRODUCER;

(j) the right to reproduce the contribution in Braille or in sound recorded form for the use of the blind;

(k) the right to use the contribution at any time for the private purposes of the PRODUCER;

(l) the right to permit recording(s) of the contribution to be used by the British Film Institute and other archives or similar bodies and made and used by the National Sound Archive for their respective private purposes.

(10)   The complete copyright in any written material provided by the Contributor shall vest in the PRODUCER but the Contributor shall retain such publication rights as are specified in Clause 10(c) hereof.

(11)   The Contributor will if requested negotiate with the PRODUCER in connection with publication in written form of the contribution or adaptions thereof and unless at the time of acceptance of this contract the Contributor declares to the contrary the Contributor hereby confirms that he has not entered into any other contractual arrangement or otherwise disposed of or restricted his rights in this regard and will not do so prior to such negotiations.

(12)   Subject to sub-clause (b) of this Clause the Contributor shall retain the right to authorise publication of the contribution or adaptations hereof.

The PRODUCER shall be entitled at any time to cancel these arrangements:

(a) if their performance is prevented by force majeure or by any cause whatsoever beyond the reasonable control of the PRODUCER or upon any breach or continued non-observance by you of any of the terms and conditions herein contained subject to payment of a fair proportion of the fee assessed by the PRODUCER after discussion with you for work already carried out;

(b) for any other reason subject to payment of the full fee under this contract or to the offer of an alternative date(s) as the PRODUCER shall decide and you shall have no further claim whatsoever upon the PRODUCER. Any termination under this clause shall be without prejudice to any other rights or remedies of the PRODUCER.

(13)   The programme titles and the date and time of transmission of the programme(s) stated overleaf may be changed at the discretion of the PRODUCER.

(14)   The PRODUCER shall not be liable to the Contributor or to his legal personal representatives for any loss damage or injury to the person or property of the Contributor arising from this engagement unless caused by negligence of the PRODUCER as the case may be or his respective servants.

(15)   The Contributor shall be responsible for ensuring that any equipment (including any exhibit(s)) supplied by him is safe and complies with the PRODUCER's safety requirements.

(16)   All fee(s) specified herein shall unless otherwise stated be exclusive of VAT if this is relevant.

(17)   Any notice required to be given to the Contributor shall be given in writing to the Contributor at the address shown in the attached offer of engagement. The Contributor should retain the Top Copy of this Agreement and return the Acceptance Copy to the PRODUCER at its address shown in the attached offer of engagement.

A.7   *Example of a short all-rights contract*

PROGRAMME TITLE: ....

....

RECORDING DATE(S) (IF APPLICABLE): ....

DETAILS OF CONTRIBUTION: ....

£

FEE   ....

IN CONSIDERATION OF THE SPECIFIED FEE(S) TO BE PAID BY (**PRODUCTION COMPANY**) YOU HEREBY:

1) AGREE TO (**PRODUCTION COMPANY**) FILMING OR OTHERWISE RECORDING YOUR CONTRIBUTION

2) GRANT TO (**PRODUCTION COMPANY**) ITS ASSIGNS AND LICENSEES THE RIGHT TO EDIT AND ABRIDGE YOUR CONTRIBUTION(S) FOR ALL PURPOSES

3) GRANT TO (**PRODUCTION COMPANY**) ALL BROADCASTING, PUBLISHING AND ALL OTHER RIGHTS IN ALL MEDIA WHETHER IN EXISTENCE NOW OR YET TO BE INVENTED IN THE WHOLE OR ANY PART OF YOUR CONTRIBUTION(S) AND ANY RECORDINGS THEREOF.

SIGNED ON BEHALF OF THE OPEN UNIVERSITY:

I ACCEPT THIS ENGAGEMENT(S) AND UNDERTAKE TO OBSERVE THE TERMS AND CONDITIONS SET OUT HEREIN.

Date ....

....

Contributor's Signature

....

Authorised for Payment

Signed Acceptance to be returned

NAME AND ADDRESS OF CONTRIBUTOR:

A.8   *Example of a licence agreement relating to film footage*

LICENCE AGREEMENT

Licence Agreement Number...

Date..

.... (the 'Licensee')

....

We have pleasure in offering a Licence on the terms and conditions contained herein. If you accept please sign each Schedule where indicated below and return one copy of the completed document to us. The other copy is for your retention.

1   a) Licensee's Production Title ....

        ....(the 'Production')

   b) Licensee's Production Number...

2   Material supplied is listed in Schedule B attached hereto (the 'Selected Material').

3   The Licence Terms and the Fees are set out in Schedule A attached hereto.

4   **Declaration** Details and the amount of Selected material used in the Production should be declared to the Licensor by .... In the event that the Licencee's declaration has not been received by this date and this date has not been extended in writing by the Licensor, the Licensor reserves the right to: (i) increase the Fees quoted in Schedule A, or (ii) charge the Licence Fee for all material supplied.

WHEN MAKING YOUR DECLARATION PLEASE QUOTE LICENCE AGREEMENT NUMBER

5   Special Clauses

.... I accept the terms and conditions contained in
Signed on behalf of the Licensor   this Agreement and the Schedules hereto.

....(Date) Signed..
                                for and on behalf of ....
                                ....
                                ....
                                (the Licensee)
                                ....(Date)

LICENCE AGREEMENT

1. The Licensor (hereinafter called 'the Licensor') hereby grants to the Licensee the right to incorporate the Selected Material (as defined in Schedule B hereof) into the Production (defined in Section 1 overleaf) for use by the Licensee as permitted in Schedule A hereof.

2. For the purposes of this Agreement:

   (i) 'Standard Television' shall mean exhibition within the Territory by free VHF or UHF television broadcast stations the signals of which are intelligibly receivable without charge by means of home roof-top or television set built-in antenna.

   (ii) 'Non-standard Television' shall mean exhibition within the Territory by means of television distribution (other than Standard Television) licensed herein as described in Schedule A hereto.

   Non-standard Television shall not include Home Video Distribution, Non-Theatric Distribution and/or Theatric Distribution.

   (iii) 'Non-Theatric Distribution' shall mean exhibition within the Territory to audiences not making any specific payment to see or hear the Selected Material and coming within the following categories of audience.

   a) Educational Institutions (e.g. universities, schools).

   b) Educational Classes and gatherings held by companies and other bodies not being educational institutions.

   c) Clubs or other organisations of an educational, cultural, charitable or social nature (e.g. drama study groups, film societies, professional associations).

   (iv) 'Theatric Distribution' shall mean exhibition within the Territory to audiences where a charge for admission is made.

   (v) 'Home Video Distribution' shall mean the distribution within the Territory of the Selected Material on video cassette and/or video disc ('Videograms') which may be played back by the use of a play-back device: and which are intended for hire or sale to the public for home use.

   (vi) 'Multi Media Distribution' shall mean distribution within the Territory by all the forms of distribution described in sub-clauses (i), (ii), (iii), (iv) and (v) of this Clause.

3. The Licensee will pay to the Licensor all the relevant Fees shown in Schedule E hereof within 30 days of date of invoice from the Licensor.

4. The Licensor reserves the right to

   (i) withhold delivery to the Licensee of any material if payments due under this or other Agreements have not been received by the Licensor.

   (ii) Charge interest at the rate of 20% per annum on all amounts outstanding beyond the payment date(s) shown on its invoice(s).

5. This Agreement does not take effect until

(a)   The Agreement has been signed and returned to the Licensor and

(b)   The Licence Fee unless otherwise agreed, has been paid in full.

6. (i) The Licencee hereby agrees either to return to the Licensor or to destroy such of the Selected Material as shall not have been used in the Production.

   (ii) The Licensee undertakes not to give, sell, grant or hire to any third party any selected material supplied in accordance with this agreement, neither will the Licensee copy or use or permit the copying of use or any part of the Selected Material in any form in or for any production other than that specified in this Agreement, nor will it use or permit the use of the Production in any way other than that permitted by this Agreement.

7. The Licensee will make available a copy of the production specified in this Agreement for viewing by the Licensor if required.

8. (i) Unless otherwise specifically stated overleaf, the Licensor warrants that it has all the rights necessary to enable it to enter into this Agreement and will indemnify the Licensee against any claim arising out of use of the Selected Material which is in accordance with the terms of this Agreement.

   (ii) Notwithstanding the above however, if notified by the Licensor in accordance with Clause 5 overleaf that permission(s) and clearance(s) must be obtained by the Licensee from contributors, copyright owners and/or any other third party prior to the exercise of rights granted by this Agreement, the Licensee warrants that he/she will obtain at his/her expense all such permissions and clearances and will indemnify the Licensor against all actions, claims, costs, damage and expenses incurred by the Licensor in consequence for any breach of non-observance of this warranty or any other warranty or undertaking given in this Agreement.

9. The Licensee warrants that the Production will not contain anything likely to bring the Licensor or the BBC into disrepute or be defamatory of any person or corporation.

10. The Licensee undertakes not to assign to a third party any rights acquired under the terms of this Agreement unless previously authorised in writing by the Licensor to do so.

11. The Licensee undertakes to examine all technical material upon receipt and to notify the Licensor in writing within 30 days of receipt of any defect that prevents use.

12. (i) If in the opinion of the Licensor the performance of the Agreement shall for reasons arising from a state of war, civil commotion, lock out strike, industrial action, breakdown of equipment, natural disaster or other abnormal circumstances become impractical or if the complete performance of the Agreement shall be prevented by force majeure or any other cause beyond the reasonable control of the Licensor or the Licensee, the Licensor may forthwith determine the Agreement. In this event the Licensee shall have no claim upon the Licensor for renumeration expenses, costs, damages or otherwise, except for such proportion of the total fees as may already have been paid to the Licensor by the licensee under the terms of payment in the Agreement.

(ii) Nothing in sub-clause (i) of the Clause shall entitle the Licensee to any remuneration, expenses, costs or damages from the Licensor if the impossibility of the performance of the Agreement shall arise from the default of the Licensee.

13. This Agreement may be terminated and the rights granted hereunder may be withdrawn by the Licensor if the Licensee commits any material breach of the provision of the Agreement and does not take steps to remedy such breach within thirty days of receiving written notice from the Licensor so to do provided that, if the Licensee advises the Licensor during such thirty days that a dispute or disagreement exists as to such alleged breach, this Agreement shall not be cancelled, but in such event the Licensor and the Licensee agree in good faith promptly to utilise their efforts to resolve same.

14. Any termination of this Agreement shall not cancel any indebtedness of the Licensee to the Licensor.

15. Nothing within this Agreement will constitute a partnership.

16. This Agreement shall be governed by and interpreted in accordance with the Laws of England and be subject to the jurisdiction of the English Courts.

SCHEDULE A

attached to Licence Agreement

Number..

Date...

The Licence Terms

1. Rights Granted
2. Number of Transmissions
3. Territory
4. Licence Period
5. Additional Option
6. The Additional Option in (5) above expires 90 days after the date of this Agreement unless previously exercised in writing.
7. Special conditions

Fees

8. Licence Fee
9. Technical Costs
10. Research Fees
11. Viewing Fees
12. Other Fees

....
Signed on behalf of the Licensor

I accept the terms and conditions contained in this Agreement and the Schedules hereto.

.... (Date)

Signed...

for and on behalf of ....

....

....

(the Licensee)

....(Date)

SCHEDULE B

attached to Licence Agreement

Number...

Date..

The Selected Material

....   I accept the terms and conditions contained in
Signed on behalf of the Licensor   this Agreement and the Schedules hereto.

.... (Date)   Signed...

for and on behalf of ....

....

....

(the Licensee)

....(Date)

A.9   *Example of definitions relating to television and video*

DEFINITIONS

1.   **Standard Television** shall mean conventional free VHF or UHF broadcast television transmitted by means of over the air standard television signals.

2.   **Non-Standard Television** means all forms of television distribution whether now existing or developed in the future (other than (1) (3) and (4) and theatric distribution) and however transmitted or delivered and shall include, but not be limited to:

   basic cable television, subscription television, multi-distribution service, direct broadcast, broadcasting systems for any or all of which service subscribers make regular payments related specifically to programmes scheduled for exhibition, satellite and transmission via non-standard television delivery systems to closed circuit television systems i.e. hotels. All of the systems whether interalia, pay-per-view, licence, rental, sale, free.

3.   **Non-Theatric Distribution** shall mean sale hire lease or licensing in all formats and by all means of the technologies now in existence or hereafter discovered including but not limited to film videograms closed circuit television education cable and off air videotaping subject to the agreement of relevant unions guilds and copyright and other rights holders of transmission (including satellite transmissions) for exhibition to non-paying audiences in all educational institutions and other organizations of an educational cultural religious charitable or social nature of an institutional or commercial nature (when the purpose of the exhibition is informative or educational).

4.   **Videograms** shall mean video cassettes video discs and any other devices for reproducing visual images and sounds which may be played back by the use of a playback device and intended for sale to the public for private home use only.

A.10   *Interactive rights definition*

This model clause could be used in an agreement either commissioning or clearing 'Interactive Rights', thereby allowing the producer to include material in formats or systems allowing the user to view or otherwise select the programme elements out of sequence. It could be amended to license programming for interactive use. Unless otherwise stated in the contract, 'Interactive Rights' should not be taken to include other rights such as 'Home Video' or 'Non-Theatric' distribution.

Interactive rights shall mean the right to make use of the contribution/materials here licensed, in whole or in part, by all means and in all media in existence or yet to be invented in (including but not limited to CD-ROM, CD-I, disks, cassettes, cable and satellite systems and any other media capable of carrying digital and/or analogue information) for synchronous or dissynchronous use by means of interactive playback systems or devices which enable the user to select among programme elements, singly or in combination.

A.11   *Moral rights waiver*

In signing this contract the author waives irrevocably all moral rights which she/he may have now or in the future (including but not limited to any rights under sections 77 and 80 of the Copyright, Designs and Patents Act 1988 or any similar laws of any jurisdiction) in respect of the work produced under this contract.

A.12 *Basic international co-production agreement*

THIS AGREEMENT, made this – day of – 199–, by and between **(the producer)** and **(the co-producer)**

WHEREAS **(the co-producer)** will contribute the sum of **(amount)** to the production by **(the producer)** of **(number)** colour television programmes and shall be entitled to the rights and privileges set out below.

The terms and conditions of this Agreement are as follows:

In this Agreement, unless the context requires otherwise, the following expressions have the following meanings:

"Gross Receipts"   means the total gross proceeds received by or credited to **(the co-producer)** from the exploitation of the rights granted to it under this Agreement (or any renewal thereof) less returns.

"Programmes"   means the programmes described in Clause 3 of this Agreement, including programmes which have been modified pursuant to Clause 6 of this Agreement; and references to a programme or programmes are to be construed accordingly.

"Territories"   means the territories listed in the Schedule to this Agreement.

1.   PRODUCTION OF THE PROGRAMMES

The **programmes** will be produced by **(the producer)** and are intended to be completed by **(date).**

The **(producer)** and **(co-producer)** agree that subject to the provision in Clause 6, **(the producer)** shall have the right finally to determine the content of the **programmes** and shall retain control of the editorial and production processes.

2.   COPYRIGHT

Copyright in the **programmes** will be vested in the **(name).**

3.   THE PROGRAMMES

The **programmes** shall comprise **(number)** × (?)-minute (maximum) duration and are provisionally entitled:

It is intended that the **programmes** shall be completed as follows: **(scheduled production completion dates).**

4   PAYMENT

In accordance with Clause 3, above, **(the co-producer)** shall contribute **(sum)** towards the cost of producing the **programmes**. **(the co-producer's)** contribution represents a fixed payment of **(sum)** for each **programme** which **(the producer)** will use to cover the production expenses indicated in the Budget in the attached Schedule.

The payment of the sum specified shall be made in the following stages:

(i)   the payment of **(sum)** to **(the producer)** upon signature by both parties of this Agreement. Payment shall be made in **(currency)** by **(co-producer)** to **(the producer)** by cheque or bankers order payable in London, England and free of all bank charges within 30 days of the signature mentioned above.

(ii)   **(sum)** upon the completion and acceptance by **(co-producer)** of **programmes** x, y and z, as defined in Clause 3 of this Agreement.

(iii)   **(sum)** upon the completion and acceptance by **(the co-producer)** of **programmes** l, m, n and o as defined in Clause 3 of this Agreement.

(iv)   **(sum)** upon the completion and acceptance by **(the co-producer)** of **programmes** a, b and c as defined in Clause 3 of this Agreement.

All payments shall be made in **(currency)** by **(the co-producer)** to **(the producer)** by cheque or banker's draft payable to **(the producer)** within 30 days of receipt of an invoice and free of all bank charges.

5.   **LIAISON**

Realizing that it may be impractical for **(the producer)** to be responsible to several spokespersons for **(the co-producer)** at one time, **(the co-producer)** will appoint an employee or employees to administer this Agreement. These employees shall be considered the sole spokespersons for **(the co-producer)**, and any comments relating to this Agreement for the **programmes**, both to and from **(the producer)**, shall be channelled through these individuals. **(the co-producer)** has the right to change the identity of said employees when it deems it to its advantage to do so. Such change will, however, not be effective unless **(the producer)** is notified in writing. The intent of this provision is to provide continuity of communication. Therefore, frivolous changes of said personnel will be contrary to the intention of this provision.

6.   **EDITING**

(the co-producer) agrees not to copy, alter or edit the **programmes** without the prior written consent of **(the producer)**.

However, it is agreed that **(the co-producer)** may request **(the producer)** to make American versions of the **programmes** for its purposes (modified programmes) before delivery, such modifications to be subject to the approval of **(the producer)**.

(the co-producer) shall have the right, subject to the prior written approval of **(the producer)**, which shall not be unreasonably withheld, to create or initiate, or license or otherwise authorize others to create or initiate, versions or derivative works of the **programmes.**

7.   **PROGRAMME FORMAT**

In consideration of the sum payable under this Agreement **(the co-producer)** shall be supplied with two 1" NTSC videomasters of each of the **programmes**. **(the co-producer)** may, at its discretion, make arrangements to have the said videomasters transferred into 16mm film, videotape, videodisc, CD-ROM, or any other format now known or hereafter invented.

8.   **LABORATORY AND SHIPPING COSTS**

In addition to any other sums payable under this Agreement the laboratory costs and shipping charges incurred in connection with the cost of supplying the 1" NTSC videomasters shall be paid by **(the producer)**, within thirty (30) days of receipt of an invoice from **(the producer)**.

9.   **NARRATIVE SCRIPTS AND MUSIC CUE SHEETS**

(the producer) will supply or arrange to supply **(the co-producer)** with narrative scripts and music cue sheets for the **programmes**.

10.   **BROADCAST AND DISTRIBUTION RIGHTS**

For its contribution towards the production of the **programmes, (the co-producer)** shall have for the term of this Agreement any extension under Clause 13 the following sole and exclusive right to (.................................) the **programmes** in **(territory)** **(which is defined as ....)**.

The rights given to **(the co-producer)** above shall be without prejudice to the continuing exclusive rights of **(the producer)** to (..............................) the **programmes**.

(the producer) agrees to clear and pay for any third-party rights contained within the **programmes** to enable **(the co-producer)** to exercise its rights in the **programmes**. **(the co-producer)** shall have the right to review the rough-cuts of the **programmes**.

11.   **ROYALTIES SALES AND AUDITS**

In addition to any other sums mentioned in the Agreement, **(the co-producer)** agrees to pay **(the producer)** a royalty of **(...)**% of Gross Receipts after Gross Receipts of **(sum)**.

(the co-producer) undertakes that it and any agents and licensees shall keep full accurate books of account, records and contracts showing the Gross Receipts and the calculations of **(the producer's)** royalties. **(the co-producer)** agrees to pay any such royalties to **(the producer)** in full with no deductions (save deductions for returns and deductions required under **(territory)** Law and if such deductions are required, the amounts payable to **(the producer)** in respect of royalties shall be the amounts which would otherwise have been payable had such deductions not been required) in **(currency)** within 28 days of the last day of June and December in each year. Any such payment shall include a statement of sales, Gross Receipts and calculation of royalties. **(the co-producer)** further agrees **(the producer)** shall be entitled to arrange for an annual audit to inspect **(the co-producer's)** books of accounts, record and contracts and any other relevant material in order to verify the sums due to **(the producer)**.

12.   PROGRAMME CREDIT

(the co-producer) shall have the right to insert its own logo at the beginning and/or end of each of the **programmes** only, but shall not remove any credits on the **programmes**. Any other credit on the **programmes** as produced by **(the producer)** shall be mutually agreed. **(the producer)** shall ensure that funding credit for **(the co-producer)** be included on all versions of the programmes. Language for this credit must be approved by **(the co-producer)** in advance.

13.   TERM

The initial term of this Agreement shall terminate **(?)** years from the date of the delivery of the final **programme**. After this period, **(the producer)** and **(the co-producer)** shall review the content of the **programmes** and negotiate possible revisions of same. This agreement shall be automatically extended for a successive period of **(?)** years, unless either party indicates its desire to terminate the Agreement at the end of any such period by giving not less than **six (6)** months written notice prior to the end of such period. Upon termination of this Agreement **(the co-producer)** shall return to **(the producer)** all preprint materials in its possession, and shall deliver to **(the producer)** evidence of the destruction of release prints which are not sold prior to the end of a six-month sell-off period, which shall begin on the effective date of termination and all rights granted to **(the co-producer)** under this Agreement shall revert to **(the producer)**, both without prejudice to any monies due to **(the producer)** from **(the co-producer)** under this Agreement.

14.   RELEASE DATE

(the producer) agrees that **(the co-producer)** may release the **programmes** for distribution as soon as they wish after delivery.

15.   MARKETING AND PROMOTION

In exercising the rights as described herein, **(the co-producer)** shall have the right to determine in its sole discretion all the matters generally associated with marketing of the **programmes** which shall include, but not necessarily be limited to, the creation of advertising and promotional materials save that the **(producer's)** name and logo shall not be used in any such material without prior written permission, and the right to withdraw the **programmes** from continued distribution if at some time in the future **(the co-producer)** determines that continued distribution is no longer profitable.

16.   TERMINATION

In the event that either party shall breach, default or fail satisfactorily to perform any term or condition of this Agreement, the other party may, after **sixty (60)** days' written notice and in addition to any other remedies, elect to terminate this Agreement by written notice thereof, which shall be effective upon receipt by the defaulting party.

Neither **(the co-producer)** nor **(the producer)** shall be deemed to be in default of any obligation if the cause of such default is in any circumstance beyond its reasonable control. If for any reason the **programmes** are terminated during the production stage, **(the co-producer)** shall be reimbursed for any of its contributions, unless said termination arises out of the act or default of **(the co-producer)**.

17. WARRANTY

(the producer) warrants to **(the co-producer)** that the **programmes** have the protection afforded by the international copyright convention, and are not obscene, libellous or in violation of any right of any third party. **(the producer)** warrants that the **programmes** will be of broadcast quality, and will comply with all programme specifications, technical standards, guidelines, and other policies regarding titles, production and underwriting credits for **(co-producer)** programmes and series, as are established prior to completion of production.

(the co-producer) undertakes to use its best endeavours to ensure that the rights of **(the producer)** and of third parties are observed by its users and shall notify **(the producer)** of any actual or threatened infringement of these rights. **(the producer)** warrants that it has secured, or agrees to secure prior to delivery of the **programmes** to **(the co-producer)**, all necessary rights, clearances, permissions and/or licenses with respect to all materials and elements embodied in and all persons performing services in connection with the **programmes,** including but not limited to all rights, clearances, permissions and/or licenses necessary to vest in **(the co-producer)** the rights and licenses specified in Clause 10, above.

(the producer) warrants that it has secured, or agrees to secure prior to delivery to **(the co-producer)** the materials described in Clause 7, above, all necessary rights, clearances, permissions and/or licenses necessary to vest in **(the co-producer)** the rights and licences specified in Clause 7, above.

18. INDEMNITY

(the producer) agrees to indemnify and hold harmless **(the co-producer)** and its assigns against any action for copyright, trade-mark or patent infringement or alleged infringement, or invasion of the rights of others which may arise out of the production, distribution, broadcast, exhibition or other use of the **programmes** or **(the co-producer's)** exploitation of the rights granted in Clause 10, above.

19. PARTNERSHIP

Nothing contained in this Agreement shall be deemed to constitute a partnership between **(the co-producer)** and **(producer)** and neither of them shall do, permit or suffer to be doing anything whereby it shall or may be represented that it is the partner of the other.

20. COMPLETE AGREEMENT AND NOTICES

This Agreement represents the complete Agreement between the parties relevant to the subject matter hereof. No waiver, modification or amendment to this Agreement shall be effective unless in writing and signed by both parties. Any notice or other communication given under this Agreement shall be in writing and shall be sent by airmail to the party for whom it is intended at the address specified at the beginning of the Agreement or such other address as may be designated by written notice to the other. Any such notice or other such communication shall be deemed (in the absence of evidence of earlier receipt) to be received in the (?) day (not being a Saturday, Sunday or public holiday) after posting and in proving the time of despatch it shall be sufficient to show that the envelope containing such notice was properly addressed, stamped and posted.

22.   GOVERNING LAW AND SUBMISSION TO JURISDICTION

Any action under this Agreement shall be brought in the courts of the defending party and the laws of such jurisdiction shall apply in interpreting this Agreement.

....   Date.......................................
Signed for and on behalf of (**the producer**)

....   Date.......................................
Signed for on behalf of (**the co-producer**)

Appendix B Useful addresses

The Association of Authors' Agents
79 St Martins Lane
London
WC2N 4AA
Tel 0171 836 4271
Fax 0171 497 2561

The Association of Illustrators
1 Colville Place
London
W1P 1HN
Tel 0171 636 4100

Association of Photographers
9/10 Domingo Street
London
EC1Y 0TA
Tel 0171 608 1441/5
Fax 0171 253 3007

Authors' Licensing and Collecting Society Ltd (ALCS)
33/34 Alfred Place
London
WC1E 7DP
Tel 0171 255 2034
Fax 0171 323 0486

BBC Film Library Sales
Reynard Mills Trading Estate
Windmill Road
Brentford
Middlesex
TW8 9NF
Tel 0181 758 8444
Fax 0181 847 4267

British Actors Equity Association (Equity)
Guild House
Upper St Martin's Lane
London
EC2H 9EG
Tel 0171 379 6000
Fax 0171 379 7001

The British Association of Picture Libraries and Agencies (BAPLA)
13 Woodberry Crescent
London
N10 1PJ
Tel 0181 444 7913
Fax 0181 883 9215

British Film Institute (BFI)
21 Stephen Street
London
W1P 1PL
Tel 0171 255 1444
Fax 0171 436 7950

British Institute of Professional Photography
Fox-Talbot House
Amwell End
Ware
Herts
SG12 9HN
Tel 01920 464011
Fax 01920 487056

British Movietone
North Orbital Road
Denham
Uxbridge
Middlesex
UB9 5HQ
Tel 01895 833071
Fax 01895 834893

British Pathé News
46 Great Titchfield Street
London
W1P 7AE
Tel 0171 323 0407
Fax 0171 436 3232

British Phonographic Industry Ltd (BPI)
Roxburgh House
273–87 Regent Street
London
W1R 7BP
Tel 0171 629 8642
Fax 0171 493 3667

British Universities Film and Video Council (BUFVC)
55 Greek Street
London
W1V 5LR
Tel 0171 734 3687
Fax 0171 287 3914

The Copyright Licensing Agency Ltd (CLA)
90 Tottenham Court Road
London
W1P 9HE
Tel 0171 436 5931
Fax 0171 436 3986

Design and Artists Copyright Society (DACS)
St Mary's Clergy House
2 Whitechurch Lane
London
E1 7QR
Tel 0171 336 8811
Fax 0171 336 8822

Federation of Commercial Audio-visual Libraries (FOCAL)
PO Box 422
Harrow
Middlesex
HA1 3YN
Tel 0181 423 5853
Fax 0181 423 5853

Granada Television Film Library
Quay Street
Manchester
M60 9EA
Tel 0161 832 7211
Fax 0161 839 6558

ITN Library
200 Grays Inn Road
London
WC1X 8XZ
Tel 0171 430 4480
Fax 0171 430 4453

Mechanical-Copyright Protection Society (MCPS)
Elgar House
41 Streatham High Road
London
SW16 1ER
Tel 0181 769 4400
Fax 0181 769 8792

Music Publishers Association Ltd (MPA)
3rd Floor
Strandgate
18–29 York Buildings
London
WC2N 8JU
Tel 0171 839 7779
Fax 0171 839 7776

Musicians Union (MU)
60/62 Clapham Road
London
SW9 0JJ
Tel 0171 582 5566
Fax 0171 580 0970

Ordnance Survey
Copyright Department
Romsey Road
Maybush
Southampton
SO4 4DM
Tel 01703 792705
Fax 01703 792535

Performing Right Society Ltd (PRS)
29–33 Berners Street
London
W1P 4AA
Tel 0171 580 5544
Fax 0171 631 4138

Phonographic Performance Limited (PPL)
Ganton House
14–22 Ganton Street
London
W1V 1LB
Tel 0171 437 0311
Fax 0171 734 2986

Producers Alliance for Cinema and Television (PACT)
Gordon House
10 Greycoat Place
London
SW1P 11PH
Tel 0171 233 6800
Fax 0171 233 8935

Publishers Association (PA)
19 Bedford Square
London
WC1B 3HJ
Tel 0171 636 5375
Fax 0171 636 5375

Publishers Licensing Society Ltd (PLS)
90 Tottenham Court Road
London W1P 9HE
Tel 0171 436 5931
Fax 0171 436 3986

Reuters
85 Fleet Street
London
EC4P 4AJ
Tel 0171 250 1122
Fax 0171 583 3769

Royal Academy of Arts
Burlington House
Piccadilly
London
W1V 0DS
Tel 0171 439 7438
Fax 0171 434 0837

The Royal Photographic Society
The RPS National Centre of Photography
The Octagon
Milsom Street
Bath
BA1 1DN
Tel 01225 462841
Fax 01225 448688

The Society of Authors (SoA)
84 Drayton Gardens
London
SW10 9SB
Tel 0171 373 6642
Fax 0171 373 5768

Spotlight
7 Leicester Place
London
WC2H 7BP
Tel 0171 437 7631
Fax 0171 287 1201

Video Performance Limited (VPL)
Ganton House
14-22 Ganton Street
London
W1V 1LB
Tel 0171 437 0311
Fax 0171 734 9797

Visnews
Cumberland Avenue
London
NW10 7EH
Tel 0181 965 7733
Fax 0181 965 0620

The Writers' Guild of Great Britain (WGoGB)
430 Edgware Road
London
W2 1EH
Tel 0171 723 8074/6
Fax 0171 706 2413

Index